Depression and older people
Towards securing well-being
in later life

Mary Godfrey with Tracy Denby

Help the Aged

First published in Great Britain in November 2004 by The Policy Press
in association with Help the Aged

The Policy Press
University of Bristol
Fourth Floor, Beacon House
Queen's Road
Bristol BS8 1QU
UK

Tel no +44 (0)117 331 4054
Fax no +44 (0)117 331 4093
E-mail tpp-info@bristol.ac.uk
www.policypress.org.uk

© Help the Aged 2004
Help the Aged is a registered charity no: 272786

ISBN 1 86134 642 5

British Library Cataloguing in Publication Data
A catalogue record for this report is available from the British Library.

Library of Congress Cataloging-in-Publication Data
A catalog record for this report has been requested.

The right of Mary Godfrey and Tracy Denby to be identified as authors of this work has been asserted
by them in accordance with Sections 77 and 78 of the 1988 Copyright, Designs and Patents Act.

Cover design by Qube Design Associates, Bristol
Printed in Great Britain by Latimer Trend, Plymouth

Contents

Acknowledgements

We are extremely grateful to Tom Owen and
Gill Heath from Help the Aged for their support
and help in producing this report. We are also
indebted to Help the Aged for funding the work.

Gill Herbert, formerly at the Nuffield Institute
for Health, also offered very helpful comments
and suggestions on an earlier draft of the report.

Preface

I am pleased to introduce this new research report, commissioned by Help the Aged and undertaken by Mary Godfrey and Tracy Denby at the Nuffield Health and Social Care Group, University of Leeds.

The needs of older people with depression have gone unrecognised for too long. This report seeks to review the available evidence on how older people experience depression and examine the services and support that are currently available to them. The review shows that older people with depressive disorders are largely invisible within health and care services. It is shocking to discover, for instance, that only 15%, or one in six, older people suffering from depression sufficiently severe to require care and treatment are receiving any kind of active management of their condition.

The impact of poor access to such services on the individual's own health and well-being as well as on wider society is immense. The review stresses that:

There is overwhelming evidence that failure to treat minor depression increases both the risk of ill health and functional decline, and the likelihood of a chronic course of depressive illness. (p 25)

In addition, the review argues for a radical rethink of the way in which all services are delivered. It argues that ageing is a dynamic process that can offer many opportunities for personal development and growth. Indeed, involvement in social and community life is key to older people's well-being. We believe that preventative work to address the needs of older people with depression must be planned and delivered in partnership with older people themselves.

Michael Lake, Director General, Help the Aged

Introduction

Background

This study was commissioned by Help the Aged, with its overall objective to contribute to the development of Help the Aged policy and its campaigning focus on older people with depression. Specifically, the aims of the study were to:

- review the nature and scope of the evidence on depression and older people;
- evaluate the current policy and practice response; and
- identify gaps in the evidence base and areas for further work.

Approach

The study has built on the literature review undertaken by one of the authors for the Audit Commission (Godfrey, 1998), which informed their review of services for older people with mental health problems (Audit Commission, 2000).

The initial review involved a search of the main academic databases – Medline, Psychlit, Sociofile, Helmis and Caredata – for the period 1980-98, and a search of a number of relevant journals. It drew on a wide body of literature (including American and European studies) to explore prevalence and need, while also focusing on UK studies to examine aspects such as service organisation and use.

For this study, the search was extended to capture material that had been published during and since 1998 until the end of 2002, relating to depression and older people. The database search was broadened to include as far as possible not only a medical literature but also a social science and social gerontology literature. Thus, evidence was examined drawn from longitudinal studies of ageing so as to gain insight into the kinds of risk factors that might be implicated in depression in older age.

While we sought to be systematic in our approach to searching the literature, our main concern was to be as inclusive as possible within the resources at our disposal to ensure a comprehensive picture of the nature and scope of the evidence base. Details of the databases and search terms used can be found in Appendix A; information on the longitudinal studies drawn on is given in Appendix B.

It was notable that although there is a large body of literature on some aspects of the topic, for example, prevalence and identification of the problem, there is a surprising paucity of published research on others. The evidence base tends to be dominated by the medical model, with its focus on symptoms and treatment. There is considerably less in the way of a wider psychosocial approach to research – one that explores depression in the context of the everyday lives of older people. For example, in the earlier review, it was pointed out that a major gap in the literature was a focus on user and/or carer perspectives on depression in older age (Godfrey, 1998). Yet we found no new material relating to these issues. Similarly, while for a long time an extensive evidence base has existed on the under-recognition and inappropriate treatment of depression among older people, there is little new evidence to suggest that the situation has changed dramatically. Indeed, one of the issues raised by the review is the effectiveness of this existing service models in responding to older people with depression. It highlights the need to develop an integrated approach to action that spans not only health and social care but also the wider social, economic and environmental context of older people's lives.

Structure

Chapter 1 explores the nature, onset and prevalence of depression in older age. Chapter 2 draws together evidence about user and carer needs and perspectives. Chapter 3 considers the risk factors in depression for older people and draws out the implications for service development and practice. Chapter 4 examines how people access services/support with a focus on identification and treatment at the level of primary care. Chapter 5 explores models of treatment and care and their use in specialist mental health services. Chapter 6 presents a framework and suggestions for an approach aimed at supporting a 'good life' in older age. This is seen as central in developing strategies for primary prevention of later life depression. Chapter 7 provides a summary of the key issues arising and the policy and practice implications.

Later life with depression: nature and prevalence

This chapter considers the nature, onset and prevalence of depression among older people. Are older people more likely to suffer from depression than younger adults? Is there a different pattern to depression in older age?

Depression and older people

A number of different kinds of depression or mood disorders can affect older people. As Alexopoulos et al (2001) note, such illnesses affect how people feel about themselves and the world around them, engendering a sense of the self as worthless, the surrounding world as meaningless and the future as hopeless. They can influence every aspect of a person's life including appetite, sleep, energy levels, interest in relationships, social activities and participation in social life. While everyone is susceptible to feeling low at some times, a depressive illness is distinguished first, by the intensity of the feelings, producing a sense of utter worthlessness and hopelessness; second, by the duration of the experience – the feelings persist over a prolonged period of time – and third, by the severity of the symptoms (Brown and Harris, 1978).

Depression is responsible for tremendous individual suffering and is associated with severe restriction in well-being, quality of life, ability to carry out activities of daily living and mortality (Goldman et al, 1999). Later life depression prevents a person from enjoying things they used to find pleasure in and can affect memory and concentration. It also causes pain and suffering, not only for those people who are depressed but also for those who care about them.

A distinction is usually made between major depression and minor depressive disorders. Major depression is a persistent and continuous depressed mood combined with a loss of interest or pleasure in the things that the person usually enjoys. This is accompanied by other cognitive, somatic and behavioural symptoms such as feelings of guilt, hopelessness and worthlessness; difficulty concentrating, remembering or making decisions; sleep and appetite disturbances; feeling restless and irritable; social withdrawal, and recurrent thoughts of death or suicide. Severe major depression can sometimes be accompanied by delusions or hallucinations, as in psychotic depression.

While there is general consensus on the definition of major depression (WHO, 1992, 1993; APA, 1994) there is less agreement on the nature and clinical significance of minor depression. Minor depression is thought to be a diverse group of syndromes that may indicate either an early or residual form of major depression – a chronic though mild form of depression that does not present with a full array of symptoms at any one time, called dysthymia – or a response to an identifiable stressor. While not as severe as major depression, minor depression and dysthymic disorders can still make it difficult for the person to function, and require assessment and treatment.

More recently, there has been increasing interest in sub-syndromal depression in older age – that is, mood disorders that do not reach the case level for major or minor depression (Beekman et al, 1997a; Lyness et al, 1999; Pincus et al, 1999; Geiselmann et al, 2001). Snowdon (2001) argues that symptom patterns among older people who are depressed as a result of physical ill health or disability may not correspond to those considered necessary for a psychiatric diagnosis of major depression or dysthymia, even though their distress is just as persistent and severe. Lyness et al (1999) found that older people with sub-syndromal depressive symptoms were functionally impaired to a degree comparable with those suffering a major depression or dysthymia. In a follow-up study, Penninx et al (1998) reported that older people who experienced depressive symptoms below case level for a psychiatric diagnosis were at higher risk of subsequent physical decline. Rapaport and Judd (1998) demonstrated that such people responded to anti-depressant medication and there were also significant improvements in their psychosocial functioning.

As Copeland (1999) points out, the key issue should be a focus on identifying those who would benefit from intervention. One of the difficulties, however, is that there is a myriad of definitions for sub-threshold conditions with varying duration, pattern of onset and symptom thresholds, and there is a need to develop a clearer understanding of such illnesses (Pincus et al, 1999). Such an understanding, Pincus et al argued, could facilitate the development of appropriate support strategies that might reduce the risk of more severe forms of depression.

With a couple of exceptions, most of the research on prevalence discussed below has concentrated on identifying depression that meets defined diagnostic criteria.

The identification of depression among older people does present some difficulties. First, there appear to be real differences in the presentation of symptoms between older and younger people. Gallo et al (1999) and Lynch et al (2002), for example, suggest that sadness may be a less significant feature of depressive illness in older people than other symptoms. In a 13-year follow-up study of older adults, they found that those with depressive symptoms (sleep and appetite disturbance) without sadness (hopelessness, worthlessness, thoughts of death, wanting to die) were at increased risk for subsequent functional impairment, cognitive impairment, psychological distress and death. Symptoms such as slowing of thought and activity are also more pronounced among older

people with depression, making it difficult to distinguish between depression and other health problems in older age.

Second, one of the hallmarks of depression in older people is comorbidity with ill health and physical disability (Reynolds and Kupfer, 1999; Blazer, 2000). The symptoms of physical or somatic conditions may mimic or mesh with mental health problems, making diagnosis difficult. Moreover, older people are more likely to report physical or somatic symptoms than psychological ones (Blazer, 1996). As Blazer (2000) argues, the boundaries between psychiatry and medicine become inextricably blurred in older age, posing major challenges in the construction of comprehensive and integrated service responses.

Prevalence

There is considerable variation in estimates of the prevalence of depression among older people. This is not surprising given the different ways in which it is defined and measured.

Older people in the community

The EURODEP (European Depression Consortium) study of depression in later life reviewed the prevalence of depression from community studies, excluding those admitted to hospitals, nursing homes and other institutional settings (Beekman et al, 1999; Copeland et al, 1999a, 1999b). Prevalence rates varied enormously, although all but one study reported rates of major depression below 5% and most (13 out of 16) reported rates less than 3%, with an average prevalence rate of 1.8%. Prevalence rates of minor depression varied between 8% and 14% (average prevalence of 10.2%). There was a consistent pattern of higher rates of depression among older women compared with older men (Beekman et al, 1999).

The EURODEP study suggests a lower prevalence of major depression among older people compared with younger adults. Major depression also appears to decline with age while depressive symptoms increase with age (Beekman et al, 1999). We need to exercise some caution here, however, as most studies lacked sufficient numbers of very old people and excluded those in institutional settings, so they are likely to understate the true prevalence (Beekman et al, 1999).

Prevalence studies from the US and Australia (for example, Henderson et al, 1993; Roberts et al, 1997a) have also shown considerable variation in rates of both major and minor depression among older people, which is partly, but not entirely, explained by the different measurement tools used. They may indicate real differences reflecting variation in socio-environmental and social relationship factors implicated in depression. Community-based studies carried out in the UK have revealed prevalence rates of case level depression varying from 9.8% in Nottingham (Morgan et al, 1987) through 11.3% in Liverpool (Copeland et al, 1987), 13.5% in Lewisham and North Southwark (Lindesay et al, 1989) to 15.9% from the Gospel Oak study in North London (Livingston et al, 1990). The Livingston et al study (1990), for example, found that those living alone and not currently married were more likely to suffer from depression.

We return to this in examining risk factors and resources.

Finally, the Berlin Ageing Study (BASE) provides some evidence with regard to sub-threshold or sub-syndromal depression (Geiselmann et al, 2001). This was a longitudinal study of older people aged 70 to 103 living in the former West Berlin, which included people both in the community and institutional settings. Using a relatively restricted definition of sub-threshold depression (a core symptom such as depressed mood or loss of interest as well as a minimum number of two depressive symptoms and the judgement of a psychiatrist) the study found a prevalence rate of 16.5% – that is, nearly double the rate for minor specified depressive disorders (9.3%) and nearly three times the rate for major depression (4.5%).

Older people in nursing/residential care

Prevalence of case level depression among older people is approximately two to three times higher in residential/nursing home settings compared with the community. The pioneering work by Mann et al (1984) found that among those with mild dementia and those with no such cognitive impairment, nearly 40% of older people in residential care homes suffered from depression. Moreover, depression was not related to age but to disability (particularly visual impairment and incontinence) and to social factors. Those most recently admitted and those who had come from their own homes (as opposed to being admitted from hospital) were more likely to be depressed. This could have reflected either a pattern of recovery and adjustment following a period of residence or the fact that depression might be predictive of higher mortality among older people.

A review of studies of nursing home residents (Ames, 1993) suggested that depressive symptoms (such as problems with concentration, weight loss and sleep disturbance) affected between 39% and 83% of residents, although only a small proportion (varying between 6% and 26%) had been diagnosed with a depressive disorder. The gap between prevalence and diagnosis is an issue we return to later.

More recent studies (Schneider, 1997; Bagley et al, 2000) have found prevalence rates for clinical (case level) depression of around 40% within nursing and residential care homes. Significantly, the study reported by Bagley et al (2000) was a prospective study of older people entering nursing and residential care where initial interviews were carried out within 14 days of admission. For these older people, depression was evidently a factor in their admission to long-term care.

Summary

Depression is one of the most prevalent conditions in later life and a significant health problem among older people. It causes considerable pain and suffering and impacts on physical health and functioning, well-being, quality of life and mortality.

Prevalence estimates of depression in older people vary, depending on the definition used, the population studied and the methods used to identify cases.

Within community settings, the prevalence of major depression averages 1.8%; that of minor depression, 11.2%, with an average prevalence of 13.3% for all case level depression. It is important to note, however, that there is considerable variation in rates of both major and minor depression. If one includes sub-threshold or sub-syndromal depression – and there are strong clinical arguments to do so – prevalence doubles.

Prevalence of depression for older people in long-term nursing and residential care is considerably higher than for those in the community. Around 40% of older people in these settings are suffering from clinical depression.

Women are more likely to experience depression than men.

Symptoms of depression increase with age. As we consider later, this increase can be attributed to age-related changes in risk factors rather than to ageing itself. It is not the process of ageing per se that leads to mental ill health. It is that older people are more susceptible to those risk factors that are implicated in depression, such as chronic ill health, disability and bereavement.

2

The experience of depression

There is very little published research on the lived experience of depression from the perspective of either older people or their care givers. While this reflected a key finding from our earlier review of the literature (Godfrey, 1998), it is notable that we were unable to find any new material over the subsequent period. Given the importance of the topic, we bring together here the main points raised in that review.

User perspectives

We noted earlier the extreme distress of older people suffering from depression. How is this experienced by them? What is the impact of living with, or caring for, a relative or partner with depression? How do people perceive their different needs?

Studies that have focused on experiences of acute and severe mental health problems among other groups of adults and their carers have documented the disruption that occurs in carrying out social roles and the capacity to function on a day-to-day basis. In a qualitative study of user and carer experiences of severe mental ill health, Godfrey and Townsend (1995) found that the most commonly described change in mood and behaviour in the period leading up to contact with acute mental health services was a physical and emotional withdrawal and an inability to carry out the tasks of daily living. What also emerged was a complex picture of the ill person and those close to them trying to deal with what was happening, while at the same time, a frightening aspect for everyone involved was the notion of the illness taking over.

The experience of care giving

The same study (Godfrey and Townsend, 1995) also found that for partners and close relatives, the period of onset of acute illness involved a gradual shift in role and division of labour. This imposed a triple burden. First, there was direct 'illness work' – surveillance, managing symptoms, monitoring and managing medication. Second, there was the coordination and carrying out of the tasks of 'ordinary life' – housework, childcare, shopping, organising the finances and paying bills – as the ill person became increasingly withdrawn, emotionally and physically. Third, there were the emotional and relationship difficulties involved in coping with the illness.

The extent of the work involved could lead to disruption or faltering of social contact for care givers. This could be on a temporary basis during the acute phase of the illness or have a more pervasive or long-term effect where friendships were broken, either because friends did not understand the illness or the care giver felt the need to keep it a secret.

Other researchers have also pointed to the social isolation experienced by relatives of people with long-term mental health problems (McCarthy et al, 1989). Increased levels of anxiety and depression linked with their caring role have also been reported in around a third of care givers (Creer et al, 1982; Fadden et al, 1987). Lefley (1987) found that behaviour problems, such as socially disruptive behaviour and social withdrawal, were the main factors in carer burden in respect of adults with mental health problems. The most common needs reported by care givers in adult mental health related to the sharing of information about diagnosis, treatment options, outcomes and prognosis; practical help, and emotional support (McCarthy et al, 1989; Godfrey and Townsend 1995).

We could identify only a small number of studies that have focused on carers of older people with a depressive illness. Liptzin et al (1988) examined the burden experienced by carers of older people with dementia and depression who had been hospitalised. They found similar levels of burden among both groups of care givers. Moreover, while most depressed older people had improved clinically after six months, carers continued to report high levels of burden.

Hinrichsen and colleagues (Hinrichsen et al, 1992; Hinrichsen and Zweig, 1994; Hinrichsen and Hernandez, 1995) have carried out a number of studies on care giving in later life, depression, and the effectiveness of intervention strategies to support such carers. The united study (Hinrichsen et al, 1992) involved 150 spouse and adult child care givers and their depressed relatives. Older people were interviewed shortly after their admission to acute in-patient care, and then they and their primary care givers had a further interview at six months and one year following this admission. A fifth of these older people suffered from a psychotic depressive illness. All lived at home prior to their admission and had been severely depressed for an average of 24 weeks. Just over half the care givers were spouses.

Employing both standardised measures of burden (for example, the Care Giving Burden Interview, Symptoms Checklist) and open-ended questions, care givers were asked to identify the difficulties and rewards of care giving. The main problems experienced were interpersonal (26% of responses). These included difficulties in attempting to motivate their ill relative; finding that help offered was rejected or perceived as inadequate; uncertainty about how to respond; loss of intimacy or companionship, and changes in role relationships. Other problem areas involved practical difficulties (24% of responses) and included competing responsibilities, financial strain and dealing with dependency needs. The third group of problems were emotional (18% of responses), encompassing feelings of helplessness, concern or guilt and emotional

distress. The fourth group of problems arose from the behavioural symptoms of the illness (16% of responses), such as their relatives' reduced levels of activity or interest, demanding or complaining behaviour, negativity, hostility, and sleep and appetite changes.

It seemed then, that what caused most difficulties were the emotional and practical impacts of the illness and its effect on interpersonal relationships, and not the affective or cognitive symptoms. Fewer carers identified rewards of care giving but these focused primarily on their relationship with the depressed person (45%), their positive sense of self (32%) and their relationship with others (21%) as an outcome of their caring role (Hinrichsen and Zweig, 1994).

A subsequent paper (Hinrichsen and Hernandez, 1995) reported that while neither demographic characteristics of the user (age, gender, social class) nor clinical features of the illness (severity or past history of depression) were related to clinical outcome at one year, specific family factors were linked with outcome. Where care givers displayed more psychiatric symptoms themselves (for example, depression or anxiety), had poorer physical health, and reported more problems in caring for their depressed relatives, the latter were less likely to recover. Thus, the role of family relationships and support appears crucial in predicting outcome among older people with depression.

Drawing on this research and their clinical experience, Hinrichsen and Zweig (1994) consider that family members have a critical role to play in the diagnostic process and that they should be involved in treatment. They consider that assessment and therapeutic interventions need to take account of, and respond to, interpersonal difficulties between the ill person and their care giver.

The research carried out by Hinrichsen and colleagues did not explore the actual content of care giving. However, a small qualitative study by Farran et al (1998) with carers of older people with depression did. Care provided was primarily concerned with instrumental tasks (shopping, paying bills, preparing meals, running errands), with few requiring help with personal care. The other main form of support related to the ill person's emotional needs – that is, offering reassurance and tolerance, and managing cognitive and behavioural symptoms. As with the evidence on caring in adult mental health, care givers here reported loss of social networks as a consequence of the illness, particularly in respect of friends and neighbours. The main areas of unmet need identified to enable them to continue caring were help with the tasks associated with care giving, more stimulation for their relative, and to be able to get out themselves.

It is evident that considerably more work is required to increase understanding of user and carer perspectives on mental health problems of older people and the type of services and interventions to support them. The evidence currently available suggests that the needs of carers of older people with functional mental health problems are broadly similar to those reported for carers of other adults with such problems. But further insight is needed into the detail. More understanding is also required of the coping strategies that seem most effective for care givers, and the relative benefits of different types of interventions specifically for older people with functional mental illnesses.

Summary

The limited research that exists on older people with depression points to the considerable suffering that is caused: the inability to manage the tasks of daily living, and the disruption and contraction of social relationships. For care givers, the 'work of caring' involves direct illness work – specifically surveillance, emotional support or reassurance, and managing and monitoring symptoms and medication. It also encompasses instrumental tasks – housework, shopping, organising the finances and paying bills, as well as dealing with the emotional and relational impacts of the illness and its effect on interpersonal relationships.

Care giving does not imply fixed roles, relationships and tasks but involves changes in roles and tasks during different phases of the illness. It appears also that the care giving context and interpersonal atmosphere are crucial factors in patient outcome. In this framework, responding to the needs of

carers – for information, emotional support, development of coping strategies, practical help – is key to providing an appropriate therapeutic response to the needs of the ill person. The fact too that the main practical tasks of care giving for older people with depression relate to instrumental and not to personal care tasks has implications for the kind of domiciliary support services that may be helpful.

3

Risk and vulnerability

A framework for understanding risk

In this chapter, we explore the evidence relating to risk factors in depression for older people. Conversely, we also seek to identify those protective factors or resources – psychological, social and environmental – that may reduce risk or support recovery among those who are depressed.

In seeking to understand older people's vulnerability to depression and therefore the services and interventions that might reduce risk and promote recovery, it is useful to draw on the aetiological model of depression developed by Brown and colleagues (Brown and Harris, 1978; Brown, 1992). They suggest three main sets of factors that play a role in bringing about a depressive disorder or affecting its severity and course:

- *Provoking agents or stressors:* factors that are capable of producing a depressive disorder. They include life events occurring at a particular point in time (for example, bereavement); a major psychosocial difficulty present over a prolonged period of time (for example, caring for a disabled relative) or a severe, threatening event (for example, sudden illness or disability of someone close). In these cases, it is not simply a matter of the specific events themselves but the meaning they have for the individual. These provoking agents influence when the depression is likely to occur.

- *Vulnerability or protective factors:* that leave a person vulnerable to the effects of a current provoking agent or alternatively, reduce the risk of developing depression. For example,

the presence of someone who offers a close, confiding relationship may mitigate or ameliorate the impact of a major loss. While Brown and Harris focus primarily here on the life circumstances of the individual, they also suggest that background social factors such as class may be associated with vulnerability. Such an association, they point out, assumes common, underlying experiences, and this needs to be explored.

- *Symptom formation factors:* unlike provoking agents or vulnerability factors, they do not increase the risk of depression but have an impact on its form and severity. For example, the loss of close friends may increase the risk of depression for an older person but whether that loss occurs through death, illness or disability may affect the persistence and severity of the depression.

For Brown and Harris, it is the interaction between these sets of factors, including their meaning for an individual, which gives rise to a depressive illness or impacts on recovery. The model therefore seeks to explain why the presence of risk factors alone does not lead to depression. It raises the question as to why some people cope with stressors while others do not. It also acknowledges that people vary in the vulnerability/protective factors or resources available to them (psychological, interpersonal, social and environmental), which might protect against risk or support recovery.

Building up a clear understanding of risk and vulnerability in later life depression will facilitate the development of strategies that are targeted at those who are most at risk on the one hand, and provide the basis for constructing a preventative approach on the other. In the discussion below, we review the evidence on risk, vulnerability and coping relating to depression in older people. The discussion is organised around the following:

Background risk factors
- Age, gender, ethnicity
- Socioeconomic situation

Stressors
- Previous experience of depression
- Experience of loss, such as ill health or disability
- Specific life events, including bereavement
- Key points of transition in the ageing process, such as retirement

Protective/vulnerability factors
- Personal/psychological
- Social relationships and social support
- Environmental factors

Background risk factors

Age

We noted in Chapter 1 that while major depression declined with age, depressive symptoms, albeit contributing to functional decline, increased.

However, the precise relationship between age and depression is both complex and controversial (Jorm, 2000). Although the consensus from European, American, Canadian and Australian studies is that there is a lower prevalence of major depression among older people compared with younger adults (Bland et al, 1988; Weissman et al, 1985; Henderson et al, 1993), this is only part of the picture. There is considerable evidence that depressive symptoms increase with age, although it appears that this is attributable to age-related changes in risk factors rather than to ageing itself (Roberts et al, 1997a; Beekman et al, 1999).

The cross-sectional study of 5,000 older people in Liverpool, carried out by Copeland et al (1999c) and using AGECAT to measure cases and sub-cases, found that age was not associated with depression in later life, but being a woman, widowed, having alcohol problems,

physical disability, ill health and dissatisfaction with life, were. Importantly here, the sub-cases shared many of the risk factors for depression as the cases, suggesting that prevention strategies would need to be attempted at an early stage, before the full development of case level depression.

Longitudinal studies offer further clarification of these issues. Henderson et al (1997) explored outcomes of depression in a community sample of people aged over 70, after three to four years. They found that increasing age was not related to case level depression, the level of depressive symptoms or change in depressive symptoms. Instead, predictors of depression at follow-up were deterioration in health and activities of daily living, poor current health, poor social support, low current activity levels and high service use. Importantly too, Henderson et al found that depressive symptoms were not a risk factor for subsequent dementia or cognitive decline. The Berlin Ageing Study (BASE) – a longitudinal, multidisciplinary, intensive study of a representative sample of older people aged 70-100+ – drew similar conclusions (Wernicke et al, 2000). Both of these studies included older people in long-term care settings.

A further paper within the BASE is also of interest here. Focusing on well-being among the 'younger old' (aged 70-84) and the 'older old' (85+), Smith et al (2002) found that the 'younger old' reported consistently higher positive well-being than the 'older old' (life satisfaction, satisfaction with ageing and feeling good about oneself). The main sources of positive well-being were social relationships and social participation. Conversely, lower positive well-being in advanced older age reflected the impact of ill health and disability on relationships and valued activities. There was no evidence that reduced well-being or prevalence of diagnosed major depression increased with ageing per se. The authors concluded that:

Poor health in very old age may eventually be an overwhelming factor that either dampens the capacity to experience positive emotions or limits opportunities for such experiences. Social participation and social contacts, for example, are prime sources of positive affect. Clearly, older adults who have great difficulty seeing and hearing and rarely move beyond the confines of their place of residence are at risk in terms of reduced opportunity for social contacts. The oldest old typically have to rely on the 'social world' to come to them. (Smith et al, 2002, p 729)

Similar findings emerged from our qualitative study of older people in two localities (Godfrey et al, 2004). We found that for those who were unable to get out and about independently, their sense of well-being was sustained by the degree to which they continued to do things that were pleasurable to them; their 'social world' came to them, and/or they were able to get out with the support of family and friends. We return to these issues later in considering the implications for prevention.

Gender

Women are more likely to experience depression than men. They generally report more depressive symptoms than men at younger ages and continue to do so in later life (Linzer et al, 1996; Prince et al, 1999a ; Zarit et al, 1999). There is some evidence from the EURODEP study (Prince et al, 1999b) that the presentation of depressive symptoms in women differs from that in men. Two sets of factors were distinguished in the depression scale used to measure symptoms (EURO-D scale). These related to affective suffering (low mood, tearfulness, wishing death and sleep) and motivation (enjoyment, interest and concentration). While women experienced nearly double the rate of depressive symptoms than men, this was primarily accounted for by their increased rates of affective symptoms.

Women differ from men in another respect. Whereas prevalence of depression is lower among those who never married compared with those who are separated, widowed or divorced, marriage protects men but is a risk factor for women (Prince et al, 1999a). This is consistent with observations from several studies in which married older men cite their wife as their main confidante, whereas women more often cite a friend outside the home. For men too, the risk of onset of depression over a five-year follow-up (Kivela et al, 1996) was higher for those who

reported poor emotional relations with their wives.

It is not clear why there is a higher prevalence of depression among older women. One explanation is that it reflects women's higher prevalence of disability as a result of problems such as arthritis, which also tend to be accompanied by chronic pain (Bird and Parsloe, 2002). Another possible explanation is that older men suffering from depression have a higher mortality risk than women experiencing depression. In a six-year follow-up, Schoevers et al (2000) found that while major depression increased mortality among both men and women, older men were more at risk of death than women, associated not only with a major depressive illness but also with mild depressive symptoms.

Ethnicity

Research in the US found particularly high rates of major depression (11.5%) in a multi-ethnic sample of older, inner-city adults who were also poor (Arean et al, 1997, quoted in Unutzer et al, 1999).

In Britain, research interest in the health of minority ethnic elders is in its infancy (Smaje, 1995). It is likely that older people from minority ethnic communities may be at increased risk of emotional and psychological problems – the combined effect of the same daily stressors that affect other older people, their minority status, and the nature of their post-migration experiences. However, there is little research evidence available on either the prevalence or experience of depression among older people from different minority ethnic groups. From a study of mental health problems among black and minority ethnic older people in Liverpool, McCracken et al (1997) found that prevalence rates of depression varied between ethnic groups. These ranged from 13% among Chinese elders, 15% among Asians, 16% among African-Caribbean, with the highest rate among Black African elders (19%). With the exception of Black African elders, the rates are not dissimilar to those found in the mainly white, community-based study in Gospel Oak (Livingston et al, 1990). The numbers involved in the study were relatively small in each group, suggesting that the findings might not be generalisable.

Other research has produced mixed findings. Ebrahim et al (1991) found lower levels of mental health problems among Gujarati elders in North London compared with the white population, whereas Silveira and Ebrahim (1995) reported very high levels of anxiety and depression among Somali and Bengali elders in East London. Silveira and Ebrahim suggested that there may be cultural factors involved in the presentation of mental distress that pose difficulties in using symptom scales to measure depression. More recently, Rait et al (1999) have been testing out different screening methods for detecting depression among African-Caribbean elders. They found that traditional tools such as the Geriatric Depression Scale were as sensitive as a culture-specific instrument with this group. However, similar work is required with other minority ethnic groups.

Socioeconomic situation

We have already noted the higher rates of depression among older people in inner-city areas based on community studies carried out in different parts of Britain. We have also referred to the very high rate of major depression found in a multi-ethnic, poor, inner-city locality in the US.

While most studies on risk have pointed to the strong association between poor economic situation and depression, this is largely explained by poorer health and more adverse life events. However, there is also a wealth of research evidence showing that ill health and disability are affected by social class and current income. Drawing on the General Household Survey, Arber and Ginn (1991) found that within each age group, middle-class men were much more likely to assess their health as good compared with unskilled men, and unskilled men were twice as likely to have moderate to severe disability.

Considerable work is required to tease out the complex, interdependent relationships between socioeconomic status, ill health, disability and depression. Moreover, it is important to explore not only the impact of specific socioeconomic

factors on the mental health of individuals but also their interaction with the physical and social environments within which people live. We need to examine those facets of areas or localities that might impact on the experience of risk or, conversely, facilitate the mobilisation of protective factors or resources to reduce risk of depression for older people. (See, for example, Godfrey and Randall, 2003, for a consideration of the issues in respect of 'successful ageing'.)

Stressors

Previous experience of depression

Generally, a significant predictor of depression in older people is previous experience of depression (Henderson et al, 1997; Roberts et al, 1997b).

Across the lifespan, the course of depression is marked by recurrent episodes followed by periods of remission. However, depression in later life has been characterised as following a chronic, relapsing course, with slow recovery and increasingly brief periods between episodes (Alexopoulos and Chester, 1992; Callahan et al, 1994). This means that recurrences extend over a longer period of time and the intervals between episodes are shorter. In a 15-year follow-up of late onset depression (newly diagnosed after the age of 70), Palsson et al (2001) found that between a quarter and a half who were depressed at one point were also depressed at the next. What is less clear is whether this reflects the nature of the illness or the inadequacy and inappropriateness of the service response to treat it. As we will see in Chapters 4 and 5, older people are at considerable risk of not being treated, of being treated wrongly or of not being treated intensively enough for long enough, within and across service systems.

Experience of loss

Physical ill health and disability: risk factors in onset

Physical ill health and disability are the most consistent factors relating to depression among older people (Beekman et al, 1997b; Roberts et al, 1997b; Copeland et al, 1999a; Copeland et al, 1999c). Most studies have found that prevalence rates of depression are approximately double for older people suffering ill health and disability compared with those who are healthy. The importance of declining health as a risk factor for depression increases in later life, compared with younger people.

Beekman et al (1995, 1997a) found that vulnerability factors for major depression differed from those relating to minor depression. Whereas deteriorating physical health appeared to be a risk factor for minor depression, major depression was associated with partner loss and long-standing vulnerability factors such as family and personal history.

Prince et al (1997a) interviewed a new cohort of older people from the Gospel Oak community-based study in 1994 to explicitly examine people's exposure to a wide range of risk factors for depression. Their paper, based on cross-sectional data, found a strong relationship between physical ill health and depression but this was mediated almost entirely through the handicap that stemmed from illness, impairment and disability. The extent to which physical illness of older people impacted on handicap was key. A follow-up study at one year (Prince et al, 1998) reinforced these findings and they concluded that chronic illness giving rise to disablement, resulting in depression, assumes increasing importance in later life. Prince et al suggested that the mechanisms contributing to this were as follows: immobility associated with physical illness; leading to isolation within the home and limited contact with friends and neighbours in the local area; and consequent loss of intimacy and reduced sense of community, further exacerbating isolation and loneliness.

In a further prospective study carried out within the framework of the Gospel Oak study, Livingston et al (2000a) explored factors in the onset of depression. After three years, they re-interviewed those who were experiencing limitation in activity but had no psychiatric symptoms. They found that those who developed psychiatric symptoms were more likely to have experienced an acute physical illness and to suffer from frequent pain. They were also more likely to have consulted their

GP than others with similar levels of disability, but did not complain of depression.

There is strong evidence, therefore, that physical illness and disability that impact on what people can do are significant risk factors for onset of depressive symptoms among older people. The relationship is both interactive and cumulative. While physical disability is a risk factor for the onset of depression, depressive symptoms in turn lead to increased disability.

A Finnish longitudinal study examining the relationship between depression and physical disability (Kivela and Pahkala, 2001) found that depressed older people were at high risk for physical disabilities. They concluded that physical exercise and individually planned interventions to sustain activities of daily living should be included in the treatment of depressed older people. From a population-based US longitudinal study, Mehta et al (2002) found that depressive symptoms predicted functional decline in the medium term. Those with depressive symptoms who were independent in activities of daily living at baseline had an increased risk of dependence at two years follow-up. Similar findings were reported over the longer term (Penninx et al, 2000).

In another longitudinal study, Han (2002) reported that depressed older adults were more likely to experience a decline in self-rated health, independently of physical illness and functional disability. As she argues, self-rated health is an important element of quality of life of older people, so focusing on treating depression is likely to improve their life quality.

Bereavement/loss of intimates

Older people, particularly older women, are especially vulnerable to the loss of intimate relationships, for example, through the death of a spouse or partner. Cross-sectional surveys (for example, the General Household Survey) show that around half of older women are currently widowed compared with a fifth of older men, and the rate increases with age. Whereas just under a third (28%) of women and 9% of men up to the age of 74 are widowed, the corresponding figures for those aged 75 and over are 62% and 28% respectively (OPCS,

2004). It is likely that this understates the rate of bereavement over the life course. Longitudinal studies indicate that around half of women and 14% of men were widowed at least once by the age of 65 (Zisook and Shuchter, 1993). (Some of these will have subsequently remarried.)

While bereavement is a universal experience as well as a traumatic and stressful life event, the majority of older people who experience bereavement of a close relative, such as a spouse, will be able to manage the distress and adjust to a different life.

However, a significant minority, estimated at between 10% and 20%, suffer complicated grief reactions during the first year of bereavement. Complicated grief is defined mainly in terms of duration, intensity and severity of depressive symptoms. Without support and treatment, people experiencing complicated grief may become chronically ill, leading to further disability and impairments in general health (Zisook and Shuchter, 1993). A systematic review (Long et al, 2002) of risk in complicated grief following bereavement of older people found that social, relational and contextual factors were significant in explaining why some older people experienced such complicated grief and others adjusted to life without the deceased person.

First, both gender and age impact on bereavement outcomes. Bereaved men are at greater risk of death than women, particularly during the first 12 months following bereavement (Gallagher-Thompson et al, 1993). Younger old people (aged 65-74) are more susceptible to depressive symptoms in both the short term (up to 12 months) and over the longer term (up to three years) (Zisook and Shuchter, 1991; Mendes de Leon et al, 1994). Second, there is some limited evidence that socioeconomic factors also impact on bereavement outcomes. For example, higher educational status and income levels may play a protective or buffering role in respect of bereavement outcomes, although the processes involved are unclear (Byrne and Raphael, 1994). Third, psychosocial factors (for example, the nature and quality of the relationship with the person who has died) are significant risk factors in poor bereavement outcomes (Lund et al, 1993). Specifically, the more dependent

the bereaved person was on the person who died, the greater the likelihood of complicated grief. Finally, for older people, bereavement may involve multiple and concurrent losses. This increases the risk of poor outcomes, for example, where bereavement is followed by relocation and loss of or reduction in social contact with family and/or friends.

Life events

From the pioneering work of Murphy (1982), there is now an accumulated evidence base indicating that particular kinds of life events or life stress are powerful risk factors in the onset of depression among older people (see for example, Beekman et al, 1995: Prince et al, 1997a; Brilman and Ormel, 2001; De Beurs et al, 2001; Kraaij and De Wilde, 2001). First, there are chronic difficulties, particularly stress, relating to ill health. Second, there are recent negative events, such as the loss of (close) social relationships, severe illness of self or other or sudden unexpected events. Third, there is the accumulation of negative events over the life course, which leads to stress and increases the risk of depression.

In a prospective case control study, Brilman and Ormel (2001) found that severe life stress events (particularly health-related difficulties such as death, physical disabilities and hospitalisation of someone close) were associated with onset of the first episode of depression among older people. Less severe events could trigger onset in recurrent episodes. Prince et al (1997b) reported that the risk of depression at onset of a serious illness was concentrated in the first six months after the event. Using data from the Longitudinal Ageing Study Amsterdam (LASA), De Beurs et al (2001) found that while the death of a partner or close family member, or major interpersonal conflict, were associated with onset of depression, illness of a partner or close relative was linked with an increase in anxiety. They also found that being a victim of crime was associated with symptoms of both anxiety and depression. There is further evidence to suggest that the increased risk of depression as a result of crime can persist over a long period of time – being a victim of crime increased the risk of depression, even for those who had experienced it up to two years earlier (Prince et al, 1997b).

Transitions over the ageing process

Retirement

Retirement marks a key transition in the life course. While it can bring opportunities for developing new interests and relationships, it can also lead to the loss of a valued role and status. At the same time, there may be anxieties around managing on a reduced income as well as actual experience of poverty, particularly for women on their own.

Given the significance of the transition, it is perhaps surprising that we were unable to find evidence relating to the impact of retirement on depression. This may reflect the fact that the impact of retirement will depend on a number of factors: the type of work and its importance to the individual; the context in which retirement occurs; the meaning attached to it by the individual, and the opportunities available to them to forge new interests. It is unlikely that there will be a simple, unambiguous relationship between retirement and mental health.

Protective vulnerability factors

In the preceding discussion, we identified different provoking factors or stressors that increased the risk of depression among older people. These included losses related to ill health, disability and bereavement, as well as adverse life events. However, not everyone who experiences such stressors will become depressed.

We now consider why it is that some people adapt to and cope with adverse changes in circumstances whereas others develop depression. In other words, what are the factors that either buffer risk or mediate its impact on the development of a depressive illness or conversely, that increase vulnerability when one is exposed to risk?

Factors internal to the individual

The early work of Brown and Harris (1978) demonstrated that negative self-esteem and lack of social support were vulnerability factors, increasing the risk of depression in the face of a life event, at least for younger people. There is now considerable research evidence regarding older people, on the importance of such internal resources as self-esteem, self-efficacy and mastery in managing stress. There is a direct, protective relationship between self-esteem and depression (Murrell et al, 1991) and low self-esteem is a powerful predictor of sub-clinical depression (Turner et al, 1999).

In exploring the relationship between impairment and depression, Zarit et al (1999) found that it was not just the presence of an impairment or disability that determined their impact on depression but also the meaning they had for the older person – that is, how they appraised them. The effect of illness and impairment was mediated by the psychosocial resource of mastery – being able to take charge of one's daily routine and other aspects of one's life. In the bereavement literature, positive self-esteem, mastery (self-confidence and self-sufficiency), energy, stamina and strength were found to be important personal resources in the face of bereavement (Hegge, 1991; Lund et al, 1993; Prigerson et al, 1993).

The longitudinal studies of older people in Southampton (Coleman et al, 1993, 1998) found that, for most people, maintaining a positive sense of self was rooted in their relationships with their families and/or other people; in their activities, interests and social responsibilities, and in their continuing ability to control their lives and see meaning in them. As people got older, the most resilient self-esteem was that based on a broad interest in other people, not just family members.

Resilience in the face of loss has been linked with positive emotion. Studies have shown that those with more positive emotions experience higher life satisfaction and subjective well-being. Within BASE (Baltes and Mayer, 1999), the most frequently experienced positive emotions (life satisfaction, sense of well-being) reflected active participation and connectedness with the surroundings. The most frequently experienced negative emotions (anger, fear, guilt, shame, hostility and depression) were related to a lack of engagement in social and community life.

There is a substantial research literature that examines coping styles in relation to stressful situations, for example around bereavement (Roberto and Stanis, 1994; Dimond et al, 1995; Jacob, 1996; Fry, 1997). Lazarus (1999, p 102) defines coping generally as "to do with the way people manage life conditions that are stressful".

Lazarus has made a useful distinction between major stressors that reflect life-threatening events such as illness and bereavement, and minor events or 'daily hassles'. These latter are the "irritating, frustrating, distressing demands and troubled relationships that plague us day in and day out" (Lazarus and Delongis, 1983, p 247).

This distinction between major stressors and daily hassles is similar to Gottlieb's (1997) differentiation between acute stress and chronic stress. Chronic sources of stress, for example, in long-term illness such as heart disease or arthritis that are more prevalent among older people, must be lived with and managed rather than resolved. In our research on quality of life with older people across the age spectrum (Godfrey et al, 2004) we identified different types of daily hassles that were a major source of stress for some older people. These included the constant reminders of the death of a spouse or close friend when faced with having to deal with the tasks that person had previously undertaken; the myriad little things that they could either not do or found difficulty in doing because of increasing disabilities – unscrewing jars, changing light bulbs, sweeping leaves from the gutters, changing curtains and cleaning windows; and the continuous challenge of having to resolve problems that were previously taken for granted – negotiating hilly and/or uneven terrain and being able to sit down while out shopping. The frustration generated by these daily hassles was two-fold: in the absence of family, friends or neighbours, there was no obvious source of help with them, and they foreshadowed an escalation of dependence.

Findings from the Berkeley Stress and Coping Project (for example, Kanner et al, 1981) indicated that daily hassles were even more

important factors in negative health outcomes than major life events. This was explained in part by the fact that major life events, such as the death of a spouse or onset of chronic illness or disability, also cause disruption and change to the daily grind of stress. They add new demands and frustrations, many of which are recurrent and chronic, for example loneliness, managing money, house maintenance and so on. It is perhaps not surprising then that among older people there is evidence that daily hassles may be more strongly related to psychological distress than major life events (Holahan et al, 1984). The implication of this finding is that maintaining morale and reducing stress is as much about minimising the daily hassles as it is about responding to major events. Moreover, as far as older people are concerned, it raises two important issues for service providers. First, it suggests a need to focus on how people develop strategies for managing ongoing sources of stress, such as chronic illness, as well as the vicissitudes of ageing and how these might be built on. Second, it poses the question as to how services might provide appropriate assistance in managing the daily hassles.

Social relationships, social support and participation in social life

Social relationships

A fundamental feature of all social life is the existence of relationships that tie people to each other and meet wide-ranging needs for physical and emotional intimacy, personal support, sociability, stimulation and meaning. There is now considerable research evidence that links the strength and quality of interpersonal ties to health, well-being and life quality of individuals (Berkman and Syme, 1979; Gottlieb, 1987; Berkman, 2000; Smith et al, 2002). People's access to certain social ties, and particularly to the support provided by these ties, is capable of moderating stress and maintaining life satisfaction and other aspects of well-being (for example, Lund et al, 1993; Pickard, 1994).

The existence of an intimate, confiding relationship is a major factor in mitigating or ameliorating the impact of psychosocial difficulties or threatening events implicated in depression (Brown and Harris, 1978; Murphy,

1982). It has also been shown to be crucial in dealing with major stressors (Brown and Harris, 1978; Murphy, 1982; Jerrome and Wenger, 1999). Older people without confidantes report more psychological distress and higher rates of depression (Prince et al, 1997b).

The presence of a confidante is a significant factor in older people's sense of well-being and is equally important for men and women (Jerrome and Wenger, 1999). The availability of a confiding relationship has been found to be associated with higher morale and lower levels of loneliness and social isolation among older people (Wenger et al, 1996). Loneliness in older age is primarily linked to the depletion of relationships as a result of loss of functional abilities, chronic illness and bereavement (Wenger et al, 1996; Scambler et al, 2001; Cattan, 2002). It is not synonymous with living alone. At the same time, among older people, loneliness is a risk factor for emotional and physical health problems (Berkman and Syme, 1979; Roberts et al, 1997b; Berkman, 2000). Thus, there is a complex, iterative and mutually reinforcing relationship between loneliness, ill health, disability and depression.

Quality of social ties

In a cross-sectional study across four countries, Antonucci et al (2002) found that the quality of social relationships (specifically negative social relations) was associated with depressive symptoms. In a review of the evidence on risk and coping among bereaved older people, there was some indication that it was perceived social support, rather than the actual level, that was crucial in reducing depression (Long et al, 2002). Thus, it was the extent and closeness of the support (its social embeddedness) that was key in aiding adaptation following bereavement (Norris and Murrell, 1990; Lund et al, 1993; Prigerson et al, 1993). For example, Lund et al (1993) concluded that it was the qualitative aspects of the support network, including perceived closeness, shared confidence and mutual help, which were more important in achieving lower depression and more positive ratings of coping, health and life satisfaction.

Significance of social support and engagement

Longitudinal studies of ageing suggest that social support and engagement in social activities have an impact not only on survival but also on preserving functional ability (Kaplan et al, 1993; Seeman, 1995) and mental health, especially among older women (Michael et al, 2001). Higher levels of social support, specifically frequency of contact with friends, act as a buffer, reducing the excess risk for depression in the presence of handicap (Prince et al, 1998). Social support buffers the effect of depression on the risk of functional impairment (Hays et al, 1997). Hays et al (2001) also found that the protective effects of social support were stronger among those who were most severely depressed, in terms of preserving and improving their ability to carry out basic activities of daily living. Conversely, lack of social support is associated with increased mortality and poor health (Seeman, 1995).

In an ethnographic study of Somali men in East London, Silveira and Allebeck (2001) concluded that family support was the main buffer against depression among this group. Conversely, low family support in the face of increasing physical disability, loneliness, inadequate access to community services and inability to return home, decreased life satisfaction and increased vulnerability to depression among Somali men.

The type of support provided by members of different networks varies according to the relationships they have with older people. Seeman and Berkman (1988) reported that ties with children were most strongly related to aspects of practical support, while ties with close friends and other relatives were more strongly related to emotional support.

Friends are essential for companionship, emotional support, morale and reduced feelings of loneliness among older people (Lee, 1985; Lee and Ish-Kuntz, 1988). It is the interaction with friends rather than contact with relatives that best sustains well-being in older age (Bowling, 1994). The pleasure that is derived from shared activities has a positive effect on well-being (Rook, 1990) and life satisfaction (Bowling et al, 1991). However, it is friendships that are most at risk in the face of declining functional ability.

Reciprocity and well-being

A specific ongoing focus of research interest has been the nature and extent of reciprocal help between older people, relatives, neighbours and friends (Qureshi and Walker 1989; Phillipson et al, 2001). A striking feature of the daily lives of older people from community studies (see for example Qureshi and Walker, 1989; Phillipson et al, 2001) is the ties of interdependence and reciprocity that characterise relationships between older people, relatives (particularly immediate family), neighbours and friends, giving a sense of purpose and meaning to people's lives.

More generally, older people have described the benefits of helping others in terms of the sense of personal satisfaction that it gives them, the purposeful activity and the forming of social relationships. Our study of life quality of older people referred to earlier (Godfrey et al, 2004) suggests that the value attached to reciprocity is maintained among older people who are restricted to the home as a result of a disability. While recognising that the balance of support has shifted in that support mainly flows to them, their continued sense of well-being is related to the availability of opportunities to be able to give emotional, social and practical support to others. Moreover, the significance attached to neighbourliness was as much about feeling part of a wider community of concern as it was about the availability of practical support.

At a more formal level, there is a growing literature on the benefits and value of volunteering or 'befriending' by older people (for example, Barlow and Hainsworth, 2001; Thoits and Hewitt, 2001). Older volunteers have been shown to benefit through improved health, fewer symptoms of depression, greater life satisfaction, improved morale, self-esteem, larger social networks and increased altruistic behaviour (for example, Chappell and Prince, 1994; Wasserburger et al, 1996; Chappell, 1999; Oman et al, 1999). These studies found that belonging to community and voluntary organisations reduced the likelihood of experiencing depression through its impact

on self-esteem and improved access to social support, information and secondary ties. Similar findings were reported by Lin et al (1999) and Musick and Wilson (2003).

Although social support and social engagement are central in securing well-being, moderating stress and buffering the impact of risk factors in depression among older people, the precise mechanisms involved require further exploration. Lin et al (1999) suggest that there are two linked but distinct mechanisms – psychological and social.

Environmental factors

While there has been relatively little research on the environmental determinants of depression, older people have been identified as a 'unique set of ecological actors' (Le Gory and Fitzpatrick, 1992) in at least two aspects. First, the physical and social space within which older people interact becomes constricted, particularly in advanced older age, making the environment of home and its immediate environs more important. Second, older people are more sensitive to social as well as physical environmental factors within neighbourhoods and localities (Scharf et al, 2002). Thus, the design of houses and the accessibility of resources within the immediate environment (shops, services, transport) may affect the opportunity for social interaction and independent lifestyles.

Knipscheer et al (2000), following Lawton (1980) explored the impact of the physical and social environment on depressive symptoms, using data from the Longitudinal Ageing Study Amsterdam (LASA). They found that living in a more urbanised environment increased depressive mood among older people, as it was associated with more complex housing facilities (for example, flats), a higher risk of robbery, more complex traffic situations and having fewer social contacts within the neighbourhood. On the other hand, feeling able and being able to influence one's environment increased proactive behaviour and decreased depressive symptoms in older people with poor functional ability.

Summary

All the evidence around risk and vulnerability to depression among older people reveals a complex, interactive and cumulative interplay between physical ill health, disability, loss of intimates and social relationships, loneliness and depression. While ill health, pain and disability are major risk factors in the onset of depression, it is primarily the restrictions that they impose on activities of daily living, social activities and social participation that is key.

Access to intimate and supportive relationships can mitigate or buffer the experience of loss for older age in different ways. It can protect health at times when people are exposed to the adversity that accompanies stressful life events and role transitions. It can strengthen coping abilities; enhance morale and increase general well-being by enabling people to maintain a sense of continuity with self, and self-esteem. And it can meet wide-ranging needs for physical and emotional intimacy, engagement in social activities and sustaining a sense of belonging and participation in social life. Conversely, inadequate or no support, or the loss of important sources of support, can reduce the capacity to cope with loss as well as trigger emotional distress and vulnerability to physical and mental illness and functional decline.

It is evident, therefore, as Blazer (2000) argues, that interventions and therapy for older people with depression must proceed across multiple domains simultaneously – physical and psychological, social and environmental. At the same time, primary preventative strategies aimed at facilitating well-being and healthy ageing require integrated social action that focuses on and embraces the inter-relationship between such economic, environmental and social factors at the individual, social network and wider locality levels (Godfrey and Randall, 2003; Godfrey et al, 2004). We explore these issues in more detail in Chapter 6.

4

Accessing help from primary and community care

Key challenges

The *National service framework for older people* (DH, 2001) has placed emphasis on the development of an integrated approach to service delivery for older people with depression, spanning primary care and specialist mental health services. It has also noted the importance of diagnosis in the treatment of depression: "the treatment of depression involves making the diagnosis and giving the person an explanation of their symptoms" (DH, 2001, para 7.27). Given the evidence available on current practice, however, achievement of an integrated model of care poses enormous challenges.

In a discussion of the needs of older people with depression, Banerjee (1998) referred to the fact that in both primary care and specialist mental health services, only a very small minority of older people with depression were receiving any form of active management of their illness. He concluded that for older people there existed a "profound discontinuity along the pathway from disorder to recognition to treatment of depression that our current models of primary and secondary health care services do not effectively address" (Banerjee, 1998, pp 130-1). We now consider the evidence relating to these discontinuities and the reasons for them, focusing initially on primary care.

Primary care: getting through the gate

General practitioners (GPs) are the main route into specialist services for people with mental health problems and their carers. They also tend to act as significant gatekeepers to a range of health and social care services, including domiciliary care in the home, day care and respite facilities. An even higher proportion of older people in primary care settings have been found to have depressive symptoms – they are over-represented among those attending GP surgeries. Depression adds significantly to health care costs. Callahan et al (1994) found that depressed older adults in an inner-city primary care clinic made 38% more visits than those without depression over a nine-month period, leading to additional costs on the service of 61%.

There is considerable evidence to suggest that despite the fact that older people are extensive users of primary care, problems of accessing appropriate help arise at every stage in the pathway from illness to treatment.

Accessing help

Blanchard et al (1994) painted a pessimistic picture of the management of depression in primary care in Britain. They found that among older people suffering depression of such severity as to warrant care and treatment, less than a fifth (15%) were receiving any kind of active management of their illness. Barriers to diagnosis and treatment existed at a number of levels: in the interaction between the older person and the GP, in making a diagnosis and in offering treatment to those identified as depressed. Thus, nearly two thirds of older people with a depressive illness had never discussed it with their GP, and even among the third that did raise it, only half were receiving specific therapy or treatment, primarily anti-depressant medication.

Livingston et al (1990) noted similar findings from the Gospel Oak community study relating to primary care involvement in the management of later life depression. First, among older people with depression, there was a higher level of GP contact in the month prior to interview, than for the sample as a whole – nearly half those with depression had seen their GP. Second, reasons for consultation did not usually include symptoms of depression. Third, detailed analysis of a number of GP practices caring for three quarters of those with depression in the sample found no association between the proportion with depression and the proportion prescribed anti-depressant medication.

Research carried out in parallel to the Gospel Oak study (Crawford et al, 1998) combined assessment of depression in older people from a large community survey with examination of GP case notes and interviews with GPs. They found that of those identified with 'probable pervasive depression', only half had been diagnosed by their GP. Moreover, while those diagnosed were three times more likely to be receiving active treatment than those whose depression had not been recognised, levels of active management were low – just over a third (38%) of those correctly identified were being prescribed anti-depressant medication and/or being referred to mental health/social services. Further, the frequency of specific psychological interventions was also very low. Those least likely to be recognised as depressed were men, those who had lower levels of education and those who suffered a visual impairment.

Similar problems of under-recognition and non-treatment of depression in older people have been found in studies carried out in other countries, suggesting that the problems are deep-rooted and pervasive (Callahan et al, 1994; Katon, 1995). Reliance on medication to the exclusion of psychosocial interventions such as counselling or psychotherapy has also been noted (Callahan, 2001). There is ample evidence too, to indicate that even if anti-depressant medication is offered, many older people do not receive an adequate course of treatment – either the dosage is set below recommended levels or the length of time for which it is prescribed is too short (Callahan, 2001; Coyne and Katz, 2001).

But if older people are not appropriately treated in primary care, neither do they get into specialist mental health services. Most older people with depression are exclusively dealt with (or more precisely, not dealt with) in primary care. Less than 10% of those with case level depression are referred to specialist mental health services, a considerably lower proportion than younger adults with mental and emotional problems, where the figure is around 49% (Gurland et al, 1996; Young et al, 2001). We return to these issues in the next chapter. Here we focus on the barriers to access experienced by older people in primary care.

Barriers to access

In a review of the barriers to identifying and treating depression in primary care, Unutzer et al (1999) distinguish between three types: patient, provider and system barriers. In the discussion below, we focus on patient and provider barriers and return to the system barriers in the next chapter.

Patient barriers

There are many different reasons why older people suffering from depressive symptoms tend not to discuss these with their GP or to seek out appropriate help. They may lack the knowledge or information needed to obtain good care; they may be reluctant to express a need for help because of sensitivity to the stigma associated with depression; or they may perceive symptoms of depression as features of physical illness, grief or 'normal' ageing. Blazer (1993) also refers to the 'existential challenges' in later life depression – the fact that older people may see no meaning in their existence and therefore may be less likely to ask for or use treatment for depression.

These existential challenges in later life depression are both a reflection of, and reinforced by, ageist attitudes that older people themselves may have internalised. These are in turn reinforced in their encounters with medical professionals. Ageist attitudes undermine people's self-esteem and confidence, making them reluctant to ask for help, and further exacerbating their sense of worthlessness in an accelerating downward spiral. This internalisation of negative attitudes towards ageing was expressed most vividly and poignantly in a comment from an 84-year-old socially isolated man in our study of well-being in older age, cited earlier (Godfrey et al, 2004, p 99):

"I seem to have changed as I've got older. I'm not the happy-go-lucky fellow I was.... I've realised I'm an old man and being old means you don't have fun any more.... I stopped having fun and it just doesn't bother me."

The various patient barriers may go some way to explaining why older people suffering from depressive symptoms, although more likely to visit their GP than older people without such symptoms, tend not to discuss these with their doctor. However, this is only part of the story.

Provider barriers

Knowledge, skills and expertise

GPs may lack the necessary awareness, skills or confidence to diagnose and then treat older people with depression. Training and support in recognising depression has been emphasised within the *National service framework for older people*, and in the importance attached to the use of screening tools and protocols for depression in primary care (Davis et al, 2002; Gilbody and Whitty, 2002).

Programmes or interventions to improve diagnosis of depression in older people within primary care have had a mixed response. Livingston et al (2000b) developed an education package directed at GPs and practice nurses to improve the detection and management of depression. However, of the 121 practices approached to participate, 105 refused. Of the 14 practices that did participate (40 GPs) more than half took part in the training although only a minority (six) completed both baseline and post-intervention questionnaires, making it impossible to draw any conclusions about effectiveness. A Canadian study (Soon and Levine, 2002) found that notification of primary care physicians with the results of a depression-

screening protocol increased the frequency of prescribing anti-depressants and referral to mental health services ten-fold, at four weeks following the letter of notification.

The problems of recognition of depression in primary care are considerably more complex and pervasive than can be dealt with through the use of screening tools and protocols, however. It is notable that with regard to depression (in contrast with dementia) a seeming paradox is that surveys have found that GPs express high levels of confidence in treating depression in older people (Rothera et al, 2002) and also subscribe to the value of looking out for signs of depression (Audit Commission, 2000). For example, in a survey of GPs carried out by the Audit Commission as part of its review of mental health services for older people (Audit Commission, 2000), the vast majority (90% of the more than 1,000 people who responded) believed it was important to be sensitive to early signs of depression and to make a diagnosis.

Goldberg (1992) argues that more important than the use of screening tools in diagnosing depression is training in the use of more effective communication strategies. He found that GPs adept at detecting depression had a better style of communicating with patients. They listened and looked out for verbal and non-verbal cues, made eye contact, asked direct questions about psychological health and social circumstances and made supportive comments. Those better able to detect depression were also better able to manage it. They offered more information and advice about the condition and the possible ways it could be treated. Goldberg also considered that there should be an emphasis on preventative strategies for high-risk groups.

A number of reviews (Katon, 1995; Callahan, 2001; Thom et al, 2002) have suggested that efforts to educate primary care providers in screening for depression need to be combined with additional approaches that focus on improving rates of evidence-based treatment. These might include an increased emphasis on patient education and self-management of the illness, and greater access to, and joint working with, mental health professionals.

Multiple health problems making diagnosis and treatment difficult

Older people often present with multiple, chronic medical conditions in addition to their depressive symptoms, and this may impact on diagnosis in different and overlapping ways.

First, as we considered earlier, physical symptoms may mimic or mask depressive symptoms, making diagnosis difficult. For example, weight loss, sleep disturbance and low energy are common problems associated with diabetes and heart disease while poor concentration and memory loss are characteristic of both Parkinson's disease and Alzheimer's. Moreover, fatigue, high or low mood and difficulty with concentration can all occur as side effects of medication.

Second, GPs operating within a narrow band of time for each consultation have to deal with multiple, competing priorities during a brief visit. They may be reluctant to ask questions about depression and risk opening up a flood of emotion and psychosocial stressors that they feel ill-equipped to deal with and for which there is a lack of appropriate treatment choices.

Third, the presence of concurrent health problems and medication may make GPs reluctant to prescribe drug therapy because of the possible risk of side effects.

These problems pose real challenges for primary care practitioners and should not be under-estimated. As we considered earlier, it is notable that the under-identification and under-treatment of older people with depression in primary care is most likely to occur where they are also suffering from comorbid physical ill health and have a disability.

But at the same time, there are concerns that such problems reflect ageist attitudes. Such ageism can operate in two ways. First, it closes professionals' minds to the existence of the underlying depression. After all, is it not natural that older people will feel apathetic and low? Second, it may lead to 'therapeutic nihilism' – the idea that nothing can be done anyway for what is a 'normal' part of the ageing process.

In a critique of ageism in mental health, Tomb, comments:

In this culture, we have a perception of what it's like to grow old: life isn't a whole lot of fun. So when you lose a general interest in life and others say: 'what can you expect – you're 82', that is just ageism rearing its head.

Conceptualising the problem and its management

In a qualitative study using case vignettes and focus groups with primary care doctors and psychiatrists, Saarela and Engestrom (2003) provide insight into the factors contributing to differences in management strategies in the care and treatment of older people.

First, relating to the specificity and number of suggestions shaping treatment strategies, while both professional groups were agreed on the need to address coexisting physical health problems, primary care doctors tended to opt for general ideas such as 'start an anti-depressant' or 'refer to home care'. Psychiatrists were more specific, indicating, for example, a specific anti-depressant and dosage, and suggesting forms of supportive therapy that were based on an exploration of the person's resources, interests and daily routines.

Second, the groups differed in their assessment of treatment urgency. Whereas psychiatrists placed emphasis on the duration and severity of symptoms and did not hesitate to launch a treatment programme based on such an assessment, primary care doctors were more likely 'to keep an eye' on the symptoms in the first instance and less likely to apply a comprehensive treatment programme or refer to specialist services.

Third, primary care practitioners tended to rely on their previous experience of dealing with similar kinds of problems in drawing up a plan of treatment. Psychiatrists were more active in asking about the individual's personal situation when forming a plan of action.

What this research does not tell us is whether management strategies drawn out in a research context reflect those that operate in practice situations. It does, however, raise interesting questions about different ways of conceptualising mental health problems that may go some way to explaining, and ultimately finding solutions to, the problems of managing mental ill health in primary care.

Focus on major depression

Beekman et al (1997a) found that while the vast majority of those with depression were seen by their GP, treatment was primarily restricted to those with major depression. For those with minor depression, there was little or no attempt at formal diagnosis or treatment. Since the factors distinguishing major from minor depression are severity, lack of comorbid physical illness and previous psychiatric history, they suggested that lack of recognition and treatment might reflect the fact that these were viewed as the defining criteria for diagnosis and treatment by GPs. If so, they would tend to exclude those minor depressions, which are associated with physical illness and disability. However, there is overwhelming evidence, summarised in earlier chapters, that points to the fact that not only are minor depressive disorders and dysthymia more prevalent among older people, but also that failure to treat them increases both the risk of ill health and functional decline, and the likelihood of a chronic course of depressive illness.

Community and residential settings: problems of access, treatment and support

Community-based services

Recognising depression

While diagnosis at primary care level is central to the development of appropriate strategies for treatment and care of depression, the problem of poor identification is evident across care systems.

A study of home care users carried out by Banerjee and Macdonald (1996) found a high level of depressive disorders. Overall, more than a quarter suffered from clinical level

depression and half of those had a depressive psychosis. Home care users, including those with depression, were more likely to be older, widowed and living alone than the general older population. Additionally, users with depression were more likely to be living in sheltered housing and to need help with shopping. However, they were generally not being treated either in primary care or in specialist mental health services. Thus, less than a fifth were in receipt of anti-depressant medication and only 9% were in contact with mental health services. The study did not reveal how older people with depression were allocated a home help or indeed whether their mental health problem was a factor in allocation decisions. We did note earlier that one of the impacts of depression on older people was a decline in functional ability. However, as the authors themselves point out, it is a moot point whether treatment of the depression might be a more effective approach to its management than providing a home carer.

An American study of home health care for older people (Bruce et al, 2002) also reported very high rates of major depression among a sample of 539 service users. This service was offered to older people leaving hospital or rehabilitation facilities who were unable to manage on their own, to prevent admission to residential/nursing home care. Of the sample, 13.5% were diagnosed with major depression (nearly seven times the rate for older people in the community generally), of whom the majority (71%) were experiencing their first episode. Most of them (78%) were untreated. The main factors associated with depression were ill health, pain and disability in tasks of daily living (cooking, shopping, and getting out and about).

There have been few studies of depression among older people in sheltered housing. It might be considered that a move into sheltered accommodation would increase the risk for depression. It involves leaving the familiarity of home with its memories; it can often be precipitated by bereavement of a partner or close friend and/or increased disability, and it can lead to a contraction in social networks through loss of neighbours or difficulties in getting out with friends.

The Banerjee and Macdonald study (1996) found that among home care recipients, older people living in sheltered housing were more likely to suffer from depression compared with those in ordinary housing. By contrast, in an epidemiological survey of older people in Islington, Walker et al (1998) found a lower prevalence of depression among those in sheltered housing (9.6%) compared with those in independent accommodation (20.3%). While the most severe levels of disability (blindness, deafness) were relatively rare among those in sheltered housing, milder levels of disability were common. At the same time, such residents were considerably more likely to be receiving help from social services, particularly home care and meals on wheels, which could not be entirely accounted for by greater disability and more people living alone. It is possible that living in sheltered housing brought people at lower levels of disability to the notice of service providers and it was this that also explained their lower prevalence of depression. However, greater understanding of the experience of people in sheltered housing and the factors contributing to and buffering risk of depression is required before we can draw any clear conclusions.

Finally, one of the major initiatives in securing independence is the development of intermediate care services, particularly models of short-term rehabilitation. There is some research evidence that depression is predictive of a negative outcome of rehabilitation among older people for conditions such as stroke (Herrmann et al, 1998). Anecdotal evidence from practice suggests that older people experiencing depression following loss or illness may not be accessing intermediate care services or, if they do, their outcomes are poor for a variety of reasons.

First, motivation is regarded as a key criterion in securing entry to intermediate care. However, people who are depressed may have neither the physical nor the emotional energy to participate in rehabilitation programmes. Second, since the likely period of recovery from ill health and functional disability is longer where the person is also suffering from depression, short-term models of rehabilitation are unlikely to be effective in securing positive outcomes. Third, it is unlikely that unless models of rehabilitation

address both the psychological and the physical/functional problems simultaneously, they will not be effective.

A key question, therefore, is how the development of intermediate care models can sustain independence for older people with depression and functional impairments. It is anticipated that the Department of Health/Medical Research Council programme of research on intermediate care (due to report at the end of 2004) may throw some light on these issues.

Residential/nursing home care

Identifying depression

We noted earlier that there was a very high prevalence of depression within long-term nursing and residential care homes, and a somewhat higher prevalence among those people newly admitted. Even so, studies both in Britain (Schneider, 1997; Bagley et al, 2000; Moxon et al, 2001) and the US (Brown et al, 2002) provide a similar picture of under-identification and under-treatment of depression in such settings.

Schneider (1997) found that less than a third of older people, identified with depression using screening tools, were receiving anti-depressant medication. Moreover, there was considerable variation between homes in the detection and treatment of such problems. Perhaps surprisingly, Bagley et al (2000) found that qualified nursing staff were no more likely to recognise depression among residents than care staff.

Treatment of depression

There is considerable research evidence to suggest that even when depression is recognised in residential and nursing home settings, it is not adequately treated. There is very little use of psychosocial interventions (Friedhoff, 1994). Although the treatment offered is primarily drug therapy, there is ample evidence of non-treatment and inadequate treatment.

For example, the Brown et al (2002) study was one of the largest studies of nursing home residents, spanning five states and nearly 47,000 individuals, within homes that were geographically, socioeconomically and culturally diverse. The focus of the study was on the treatment of those who had an active diagnosis of depression, and it offers insight into the factors that explain variation in treatment in such settings. Only just over a half (55%) of those with an active diagnosis of depression received any kind of drug therapy. Moreover, it was unlikely to be offered at a therapeutically adequate dosage. Those less likely to be treated included the 'oldest old' (those aged over 85), black residents and those with multiple diagnoses.

Strategies to improve detection and treatment

There is some evidence within nursing and residential care settings that interventions to provide training and support to staff to help depressed older residents can give rise to positive outcomes.

Moxon et al (2001) secured the participation of care workers in a training and mentoring programme with staff from a community mental health team. This was designed to increase understanding of depression among staff and enable them to offer appropriate support to individual residents. Although the study was small, they found that staff members' identification of depression became more accurate over time (as did their ability to detect dementia), and all but one of the residents improved.

Several interventions have proved effective in the treatment of depression in residential care, including drug therapy, exercise and reminiscence therapy (Rattenbury and Stones, 1989; Katz et al, 1990; McMurdo and Rennie, 1993). Multi-faceted programmes involving mental health specialists and comprising interventions directed at all residents (activities such as gentle exercise, relaxation techniques, talks on depression, chronic pain and stress management, and support groups) as well as anti-depressant therapy for those who were depressed, produced modest but significant improvements among depressed older people and prevented mild depression from becoming

worse (Llewellyn-Jones et al, 1999; Cuijpers and van Lammeren, 2001). The Schneider (1997) study cited above also found that when problems relating to mobility, hearing and visual impairments were responded to, depressive symptoms were reduced, reflecting the interrelationship between disability and depression.

Summary

The problems of identifying and managing depression in primary, community and residential care settings are manifest at a number of levels.

First, although older people with depression are high users of primary care services, and most of them are dealt with exclusively at this level, there is poor identification and recognition of the illness. This presents particular difficulties since GPs are the main route into specialist services for people with mental health problems and their carers. They also act as significant gatekeepers to a range of health and social care services.

Second, even where depression is recognised and diagnosed within primary care, only a very small proportion of those diagnosed are offered treatment and therapy. Most treatment involves drug therapy and there is little use of psychosocial approaches, including psychotherapy and other cognitive and behavioural therapies.

Third, only a tiny proportion of those with depression are referred to specialist mental health services.

The pattern of poor recognition of later life depression, inadequate treatment or no treatment, applies also within community-based services and in nursing and residential care settings. Indeed, one must conclude that older people with depressive disorders are largely invisible within the service system.

Responding appropriately to the problems and barriers identified requires considerably more than enhancing the skills of GPs and other professionals in identifying and diagnosing depression, although that is part of it. It also

requires understanding of the interplay between
physical, psychological and social factors in the
onset and development of depression among
older people, and the development of multi-
dimensional and multi-faceted responses that
take this complexity into account. From the
evidence presented above, it does appear that
staff within nursing and residential care homes in
particular, may be amenable to and enthusiastic
about, developing and complementing
programmes to reduce depression within
their homes, with support from mental health
professionals.

Finally, it is evident that at least some of
the barriers to recognition and appropriate
treatment of depression among older people
relate to ageism. This is reflected first, in the
way older people themselves may internalise
negative attitudes about ageing. Second, it is
reflected in the practice of professionals where
it is underpinned by a belief that physical ill
health and depression are inevitable features of
the ageing process and that there is no point in
taking any action because the person is older
and medically ill. Yet, as we consider in the next
chapter, there is evidence to suggest that later
life depression can be treated effectively and
that there is no basis for a 'therapeutic nihilism'.

Models of treatment and care in later-life depression

Key issues

In this chapter, we consider two broad questions. First, what specific treatments have been developed for older people with depression and how effective are they? Second, how is service delivery organised for older people with mental health problems? The discussion is not intended to be comprehensive or exhaustive. It serves merely to delineate the key policy and practice issues in responding to depressive illness among older people.

Failure to detect and treat depression in older people has deleterious consequences, primarily the grief, despair and suffering of older people; their increased risk of experiencing other health problems and reduced functional ability, and increased mortality. But it also increases costs to the health service, as we noted in Chapter 4.

Research also indicates that inadequate treatment or delays in offering treatment lead to poorer outcomes for older people with depression. Murphy (1983) found that after a one-year follow-up, only a third of older people with depression remained well following in-patient or outpatient treatment. Factors linked with poor prognosis were poor physical health, length of illness at initial assessment and severe adverse life events during follow-up. Tuma (1996) found a slightly higher rate of recovery in his sample (45%), similar to that of adults admitted to an acute psychiatric unit. Even so, recovery was slower among older people and, as in Murphy's study, was related to duration of illness prior to treatment. The latter is a consistent finding across studies of depression in older people (Flint and Rifat, 1997, 2000).

Treating later-life depression

We noted in Chapter 4 that among older people diagnosed and treated for depression in primary care, the most common form of treatment was drug therapy on its own. The newer anti-depressants (SSRIs) have been found to be better tolerated than the older tricyclic anti-depressants (TCAs) which had more pronounced side-effects.

But key problems in ascertaining effectiveness of the newer drugs relate to the fact that they tend to be prescribed in less than optimal dosage and for too short a period of time. For example, Anderson (2001) suggests that older people may take longer to respond to anti-depressants and optimum benefit may take 8-12 weeks. In a systematic review of treatments for later life depression in primary care, Freudenstein et al (2001) found that it was impossible to draw any conclusions about the effectiveness of drug therapy for older people because the trials tended to focus on short treatment periods (4-8 weeks) and excluded many of those with other illnesses. Thus, while studies indicated high rates of improvement (54-81%), the exclusion criteria would suggest that these might not be generally applicable to people with other health problems, including older people.

Older people may not be willing to take medication for prolonged periods of time. In a report of a failed clinical trial, Stevens et al (1999) found that the older people in their study were unwilling to take anti-depressant medication for a variety of reasons. Follow-up at three and six months revealed that for the majority of those who were depressed and anxious, the illness persisted.

The use of psychotherapies for older people with depression has been slow to develop (Anderson, 2001). Moreover, much of the focus of research on the effectiveness of such therapies relates to major depression. A recent review of the evidence (Arean and Cook, 2002) found that behavioural and cognitive behavioural therapies had received the most research attention, with the focus primarily on older people suffering from major depression. They concluded that the efficacy of such treatments for major depression was compelling and that those who responded to treatment maintained improvement, at least over a two-year period.

Interpersonal psychotherapy has not been subject to the same research interest as the behavioural therapies, and much of the research here has focused on psychotherapy in combination with drug therapy. There is some evidence that for older people suffering from recurrent major depression, a combination of drug therapy and individual psychotherapy is more effective in prolonging recovery, maintaining social adjustment and enhancing the quality of recovery (Lenze et al, 2002). Arean and Cook (2002) concluded that such a combined approach was more likely to be effective than stand-alone psychotherapy.

Other forms of therapeutic intervention – brief dynamic therapy and reminiscence therapy – were included in Arean and Cook's review. Research suggests that both are potentially useful, although the evidence base is not extensive.

Most research on the effectiveness of psychosocial and psychotherapeutic interventions for later life depression has concentrated on major depression. There are few studies that have examined the outcomes and effectiveness of such treatments for older people suffering from minor depression and dysthymia, although Karel and Hinrichsen (2000) suggested from their review that psychotherapy alone may be effective for older people with less severe depression.

One of the few studies of a combined approach with older people not previously identified as having depression was that carried out by Banerjee et al (1996b). A randomised controlled trial of users of the home care service who were depressed were offered either usual care with the GP or a managed plan of care developed with the user within a multi-disciplinary mental health team. More than half the intervention group had recovered at six months, compared with only a quarter of the control group.

In exploring the risk factors in depression, we have made reference throughout this report to their cumulative, complex and interactive nature across the psychological, social, physical and environmental spheres. It follows, therefore, that treatment strategies need to respond to this complexity. Blazer (2000) for example, suggests that therapy must proceed across multiple domains simultaneously. This would tend to include strategies to maintain functioning, sustain and support social networks and improve health-related quality of life, as well as therapeutic and pharmacological interventions.

Support for such a multi-faceted approach is also drawn from studies that have examined the kinds of factors that impact on treatment outcomes. Oslin et al (2002) explored the effects of specific medical problems on treatment outcomes among a sample of 671 older people who received in-patient treatment for depression. People were assessed at entry into hospital and three months after discharge. While there was a relationship between certain illnesses and treatment outcomes, the effect was mediated through disability and pain. Chronic illness, and arthritis in particular, leading to functional impairment, pain and disability was most likely to impact negatively on the treatment for depression.

Oslin et al concluded that there was a need for interventions that focused on disability, such as physical therapy or enhanced pain management, alongside treatment for depression. Indeed, there is evidence to suggest the positive benefits of exercise in securing an improvement in depressive symptoms (Mather et al, 2002; Timonen et al, 2002). This appears to operate at two levels simultaneously: providing opportunities for people to get together and meet others, as well as the positive effect of exercise on morale and abilities.

Specialist mental health services for older people

A major change in the delivery of mental health services for older people over the last 20 years or so has been the specialist organisation of older age psychiatry. The establishment of the distinct speciality of older age psychiatry – from the formation of an Old Age Group within the Royal College of Psychiatrists in 1973 to its recognition as a Specialist Section in 1978 – both reflected and fuelled the development and provision of specialist services. From a handful of consultants in the 1970s, this number has now increased to around 400. The leading proponents of the new speciality have documented the development of the profession and the principles underpinning service provision as well as describing different styles of service. For example, Arie and Jolley (1982, p 222) define the objectives as follows:

- to maintain the mental health of older people and contribute to preserving their independence by sustaining, retrieving and enhancing function;
- providing permanent or intermittent institutional care for those who are so disabled that this is the most practicable and humane way of looking after them;
- supporting the supporters lies as a primary concern alongside the direct welfare of older people themselves.

The pattern of development of specialist mental health services has some common features as well as considerable variation.

Generally, services encompass all mental health problems of older people, including dementia and depression. The main service elements comprise in-patient acute beds and day hospital provision although latterly, community-based mental health teams have assumed more importance. They operate largely as secondary care services, relying on GPs as the gatekeepers to provision.

Alongside these common features, there are also different balances of care between hospital and community-based resources; different relationships with primary care, and

different systems and mechanisms for achieving collaboration.

An ongoing issue of concern has been the problem of fragmentation in service delivery – in respect of older age psychiatry on the one hand and social services on the other, and between generalist and specialist provision. A review of mental health services by the Audit Commission (2000) pointed to the patchy and inconsistent nature of services for older people with mental health problems across the country, specifically:

- The continued dominance of hospital-based and health-funded provision and the uneven development of multi-disciplinary community mental health teams.
- The difficulties in achieving effective multi-disciplinary assessments and coordinated care packages across health, social services, housing and other agencies.
- Separate and parallel systems for coordinating care resulting from the community care assessment and care management arrangements on the one hand, with social services as the lead agency, and the Care Programme Approach on the other, led by health professionals.
- Service fragmentation and overlaps in provision between health services (organised largely through the older age psychiatry service) and social services (with the emphasis on social care).

A subsequent audit of mental health services (Audit Commission, 2002) revealed an enormous gap between good practice as set out in Standard 7 of the *National service framework for older people* and the reality of service delivery across the country, for example:

- Patchy provision of specialist multi-disciplinary mental health teams – less than half the areas had such teams although they partly existed in a further third.
- Specialist care for people with problems such as depression, for example, day care and psychological therapies, were major areas of unmet need.
- While home care is seen as one of the key services supporting people with mental health problems at home, only one in seven

areas provided home care workers with training in mental health.
- There was little in the way of formal systems and mechanisms to facilitate the provision of advice and support from specialist mental health teams to GPs, residential care and nursing homes, and other general services for older people.

In response to the patchy and inconsistent service delivery systems across the country, the Audit Commission (2000) argued for a strategic approach to the development of a comprehensive mental health service system. This was to be commissioned and planned jointly by health and social services to make best use of resources. On the basis of its more extensive service audit (Audit Commission, 2002) it further suggested that management of the complexity of need and provision "requires good co-ordination between health and social care, with integrated teams of professionals who have ready access to a range of flexible services" (p 31).

However, a fundamental problem in the delivery of mental health services to older people is that cited by Banerjee (1998) and which we have considered earlier – namely, that only a tiny minority (6%) of older people with serious depression are in receipt of specialist mental health services. This sits side by side with the failure at primary care level to recognise, manage and treat depression in older people.

The question that needs to be addressed, therefore, is what should be the appropriate relationship between specialist mental health services for older people on the one hand, and general services that form the main bulwark of assistance to older people and their families, on the other.

Related to this is the accumulated evidence that indicates the interrelationship between depression, physical ill health, disability, poor social relationships and social support. Secondary and tertiary preventative strategies need to develop approaches that embrace not only medical treatment and care, but also integrated social action that encompasses support for practical, social, emotional and environmental dimensions of need.

Moreover, primary preventative strategies need to focus on sustaining well-being in older age through a multi-level approach. This should combine maintaining physical health and abilities for as long as possible into advanced older age and sustaining social activities and social relationships. It should also provide opportunities for people to continue to maintain their engagement in social life in the face of the losses that they experience over the ageing process.

In terms of older people with mental health problems, we can identify some of the barriers to the development of an integrated approach as follows (Godfrey et al, 2003):

- *Structural*: fragmentation of service systems, not only between health and social care but within health services – between primary, secondary and community services.

- *Professional*: the dominance of the medical model leads to: (a) the largely medical diagnosis of needs, which, among other things, ignores social causation (the influence of the physical, economic and social environment) and also the need for social care of carers; and (b) the underdevelopment of a wider psychosocial response at the individual and locality levels.

- *Status and legitimacy*: there are several issues here, closely related to those referred to above. First, older people with mental health problems have been a 'Cinderella' group, within an already neglected group of adults with mental health problems. Second, this low status has meant that the new professional speciality of older age psychiatry has had difficulty fighting for resources within the health service. Third, the low status is reinforced by the fact that this new speciality is a hybrid of two specialities, which themselves have typically been low status – geriatric medicine and psychiatry. Fourth, one effect of the need to fully establish the new profession has been the perceived importance of medical leadership and domination – with variable impact on the development of multi-disciplinary teamwork.

Structural solutions of themselves are unlikely to produce the kinds of changes required to ensure a better response to older people with depression. At the heart of any change process, what is required is a shared vision and commitment to develop responsive service systems that are underpinned by an understanding of the factors that support and sustain well-being over the ageing process. The focus of such change has to be directed not only at health and social services professionals but also at all those working with older people.

Summary

In this chapter, we have considered the effectiveness of treatments of later life depression. However, most of the evidence related to major depression, yet the majority of older people are suffering from minor depression, dysthymia or depressive symptoms that do not reach case level. Even so, as we have noted in previous chapters, older people with such various levels of depression experience poor outcomes as a consequence, and require intervention and treatment to manage it.

A significant problem with the existing service system is that so few older people get into it in the first place. This could be due to lack of recognition and treatment in primary care or to the fact that most are not referred to specialist mental health services. Even if older people with major depression do secure entry into specialist services, the problem remains of the much larger group of older people who require treatment but do not get it. Within specialist mental health services too, the degree of variation in models of support suggests considerable inequity in provision across the country. While some specialist services do offer a response that is multi-dimensional and multi-faceted, others do not.

The service policy aim seems relatively clear. It is to provide comprehensive and continuous services built around holistic assessments of individual needs – that is, to provide person-centred care. As we have seen, there are some significant problems in achieving this aim. There are gaps and inconsistencies in service provision – only a minority of services are planned and delivered jointly. Service organisation and delivery for older people with mental health problems is fragmented and lacks cohesion. At a conceptual level too, a model of action, which encompasses a bio-psychosocial understanding of causation, treatment and care in depression demands a more comprehensive and holistic response than the simple integration of medical and social care services. Such a response, moreover, will have to engage professionals and agencies that work with older people across the spectrum.

6

Securing well-being in older age

Developing a strategy to secure well-being

Repeatedly within this report, we have stressed the fact that a key defining feature of later life depression is the complex interplay between ill health, disability, loss and poor social support, as risk factors in the onset of depression and as predictors of chronic course and poor outcome. What are the implications of such an understanding?

First, as we have suggested above, it demands the development of programmes that address multiple domains simultaneously to secure and maintain recovery among those experiencing depression. Second, from the discussion of risk and vulnerability, what is also required is a strategy and service response that is aimed at sustaining/supporting well-being over the ageing process and at promoting a good life in older age. What might this good life comprise? What kinds of strategies or support might sustain and enhance well-being and a good life?

Clearly, the development of a preventative approach to secure well-being in older age has to start from an understanding of the ageing process and what people value in terms of well-being. Recent work (Godfrey, 2001; Godfrey and Randall, 2003) has sought to set out the elements of such a strategy, rooted in a socio-cultural model of ageing. This model, which draws on the concept of 'successful ageing' developed by Baltes and Baltes (1990) views ageing as a dynamic process involving both opportunities for personal development and growth, and adjustment to the experience of loss. It recognises that while older people are actively engaged in trying to make sense of and adapt to, the physical, social, interpersonal and psychological changes that accompany ageing, embracing both learning and adjustment (Baltes and Carstensen, 1996), the resources and opportunities available to them are shaped and constrained by the wider social context within which they live.

The model is set out in Figure 1 overleaf.

While there are aspects of ageing that are irreversible – we all age in body and eventually die – there is also considerable diversity in older age. We need to develop a clearer understanding of those factors that contribute to such diversity, the features of the ageing process that are amenable to change and the kinds of action that must be taken to minimise the impacts of loss and enhance positive adaptation. Such an understanding is also essential in combating the ageism that stunts and limits the possibilities and opportunities available to older people and contributes to people's own internalisation of negative images of older age.

Key elements in well-being

But what are the elements that are central to well-being in older age? There is now a considerable evidence base to suggest that engagement in social and community life is key – involvement in meaningful, interesting and fun activities, and being linked with others in relationships that meet a wide range of needs for intimacy and companionship, stimulation and enjoyment, and emotional, social and practical support. While the process of ageing can bring with it enormous opportunities for growth and development, older age, and especially advanced older age, is also accompanied by loss – whether through ill health, disability or bereavement.

Figure 1: Sociocultural model of successful ageing

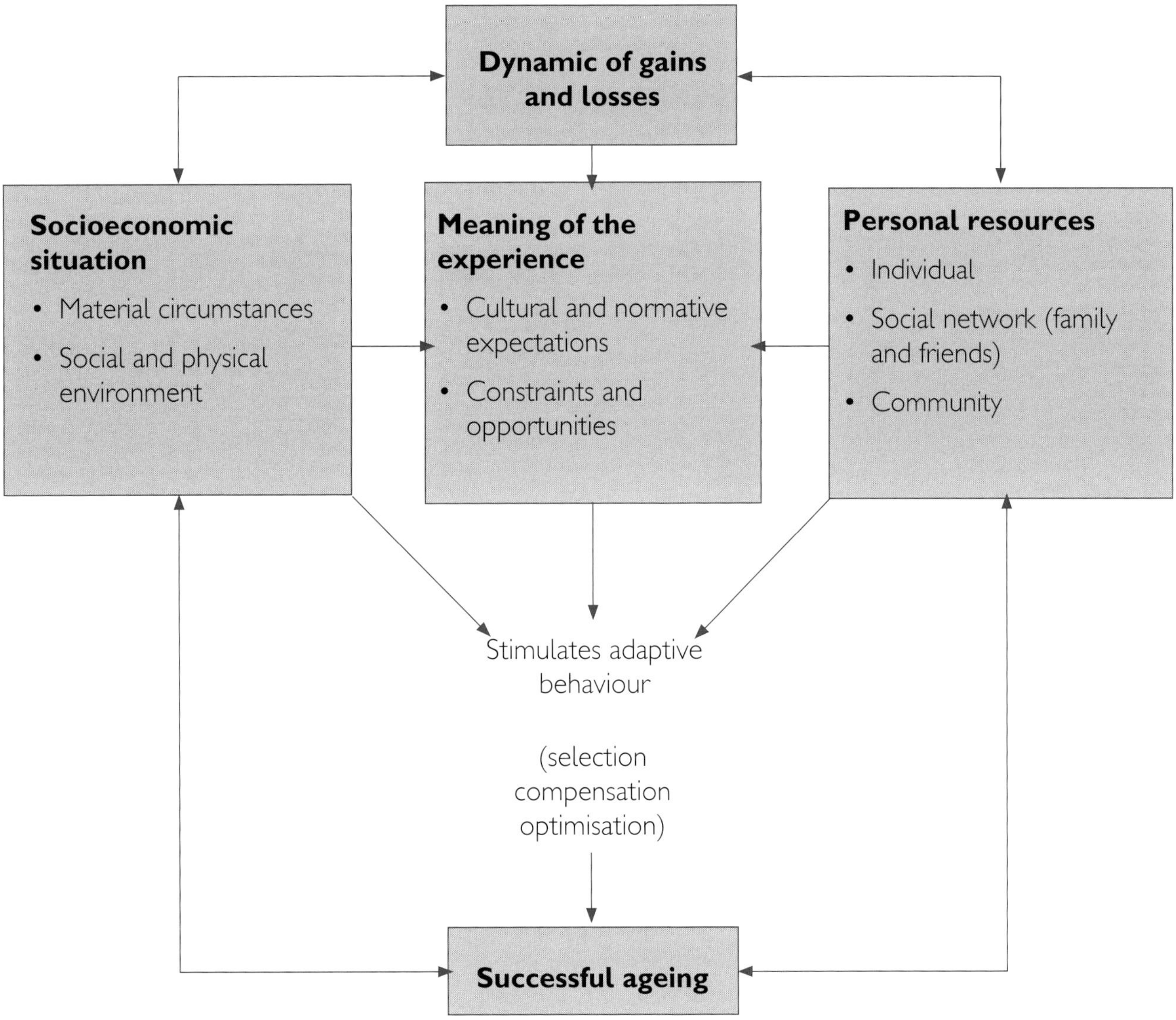

Dynamic of gains and losses

Socioeconomic situation

• Material circumstances

• Social and physical environment

Meaning of the experience

• Cultural and normative expectations

• Constraints and opportunities

Personal resources

• Individual

• Social network (family and friends)

• Community

Stimulates adaptive behaviour

(selection compensation optimisation)

Successful ageing

Where such losses impact on social engagement and social relationships, well-being is threatened.

Our own research on life quality over the ageing process, already referred to, paints a kaleidoscopic picture of 'flowering in old age' and considerable resilience in dealing with ill health, bereavement and disability, as well as anger and despair at the restrictions imposed, particularly in advanced older age.

In Appendix C we have sought to summarise the key elements of life quality in ageing that have been drawn from the literature. We have identified the threats and protective factors that either pose a risk to or sustain successful ageing, and set out the different levels at which action needs to be taken to construct a comprehensive approach to promoting well-being.

Addressing threats to well-being

At the individual level, essential to older people's life quality is maintaining a positive sense of self, engagement in meaningful social activities and participation as valued members of social networks and communities. It is the extent to which the losses that accompany old age stunt and limit those opportunities that represents the greatest risk to successful ageing. Conversely, interventions that are geared towards reducing such threats to life quality are likely to support well-being.

At the locality level, the provision of support/ resources to facilitate or enhance the social integration of older people can improve life quality even among those who are restricted to their homes or immediate neighbourhoods. In our research on quality of life, the existence of a locally based organisation of and for older people offered a range of opportunities for people to develop themselves, get involved in new activities/interests, renew/create friendships and support others. It both drew on the existing capacities, skills and expertise of older people and enabled them to develop and enhance their skills. At the same time, specific initiatives such as befriending and the organisation of small neighbourhood groups for people with disabilities meant that their social worlds could be sustained over a longer period of time, despite the restrictions imposed by disability.

There are threats to well-being as people get older that demand action at local authority and national government level. This would need to include the construction of environments that sustain people in older age, by addressing disadvantage on the one hand, and developing the capacities of individuals and groups across generations to secure healthy communities, on the other. It is evident that the quality of the physical environment contributes to older people's sense of dissatisfaction with and alienation from the places in which they live. The experience of being a victim of crime is a risk factor in the development of a depressive illness – the fear of crime can keep people inside their homes, reluctant to move beyond their immediate locality. Moreover, disability and loss of health in older age cannot simply be explained by age-related factors. Differential access to economic and social resources over the life course, which persist into older age, also affect health and functional ability. Reducing inequality is therefore essential in promoting a good life in older age.

Developing a preventative approach

There are certain points of transition across the ageing process and particular types of losses that increase vulnerability and threaten well-being, for example retirement, ill health and bereavement. In very old age, not only are people more likely to experience loss but the losses are cumulative and interactive. At the same time, their resources to cope with loss are likely to be suffering depletion. Similar themes emerged in our discussion of risk factors in depression (Chapter 3).

There is a need to consider the development of a combined approach to prevention. This would require, first, a consideration of specific interventions and programmes that would reduce susceptibility to particular types of risk factors; and second, directing particular attention on those experiencing a multiplicity of risk factors in interaction.

The evidence base and ideas presented here offer a framework for developing a preventative approach – one that addresses, severally and together, risk and resources at the individual, community and national levels in the context of a partnership with older people themselves. It suggests a way of thinking about the kinds of services and support that would form the basis for an integrated and comprehensive service response to support well-being in older age, and to address those risk factors that make older people vulnerable to depression.

7

Summary and conclusions

Nature and scale of later-life depression

Depression is one of the most prevalent health problems experienced by older people. While there is variation in prevalence rates, the consensus suggests that some 13% to 15% of older people living in the community suffer clinical level depression, although prevalence doubles if one includes people with depressive symptoms at sub-case level. Indeed, there are strong clinical arguments to include a wider definition of depression since there is clear evidence that older people who experience depressive symptoms have similar poor outcomes in terms of mortality and morbidity as those with case level depression. They are also high users of general health and social care services.

The prevalence of depression is considerably higher within permanent residential and nursing home settings compared with the community (around 40%). It appears also that depression is a significant factor in admission to residential/nursing homes. Several possible explanatory factors may be involved. First, because of the depression, the person may have little confidence in his/her ability to manage at home and therefore seeks the comfort of a safe, secure environment. Second, the depression may have contributed to ill health and disability, which has then precipitated an admission. Third, the experience of a sudden acute episode of ill health requiring hospital admission may have given rise to a depressive illness, which in turn contributes to poor recovery and inability to resume day-to-day tasks. In each case, greater attention to the underlying stressors provoking the depressive episode as well as specific support and treatment to address both the

depression and the underlying stressors, may avoid some admissions to long-term care.

The experience of the illness

There is a considerable amount of information available about depression from the perspective of clinicians and epidemiologists. However, there is a dearth of experiential understanding of the illness from the perspective of the older person or those close to them. What we do know is that depression pervades every aspect of the person's life, threatening self-identity and self-esteem as well as impacting on physical health and well-being, social relationships, social activities and the ability to carry out the tasks of everyday living.

For friends and relatives as well, the illness evokes considerable distress and gives rise to significant 'illness work'. For care givers, it appears that it is not just the physical and practical demands of caring that cause stress but interpersonal difficulties related to inability to motivate their relative to do anything, the loss of intimacy and companionship in the face of withdrawal of the ill person and their feelings of hopelessness and powerlessness. This serves to underscore the crucial role played by family members in the assessment and treatment process, and the need to involve them directly in action or planning.

Risk and vulnerability

In exploring risk and vulnerability to depression among older people, a number of key themes emerge.

First, later life depression is neither an inevitable nor an irreversible feature of the ageing process. For older people – to a greater extent than for younger adults – physical ill health, pain and disability are the most consistent risk or provoking factors in depression. However, what are decisive are not ill health and/or disability per se but the restrictions that these impose on people's engagement in social activities and social relationships. Loss of an intimate or partner as a result of bereavement is also a risk factor in depression. This appears to be more significant for major than for minor depression, especially when linked with long-standing vulnerability factors such as family and personal history. Other risk factors include adverse life events such as chronic physical difficulties; the daily hassles that are an ever present reminder of loss or increasing disability; sudden, unexpected events like an acute, life-threatening illness and hospitalisation; or being a victim of crime.

Second, and equally relevant, is the enormous resilience of people over the ageing process in the face of stress. Not all those who experience loss go on to develop a depressive illness. It depends on the meaning of the loss for the older person. It also relates to the person's degree of vulnerability when exposed to risk or, conversely, their access to resources or protective factors that either buffer stress or mediate its impact on the development of a depressive illness. Important protective factors internal to the individual are self-esteem, a positive sense of self and mastery. Significant also is whether people are enmeshed within reciprocal and interdependent relationships that meet wide-ranging needs for physical and emotional intimacy, engagement in social activities and sustaining a sense of belonging and participation in social life.

Third, all the evidence suggests that there is a complex interplay between risk and vulnerability factors in depression, ill health or disability that makes it difficult to get out and about. This leads to reduced social activity and loss of friends, giving rise to social isolation and depression in an accelerating a downward spiral of ever decreasing engagement. It is clear therefore that effective strategies for the management and treatment of depression must, as Blazer (2000, p 157) expressed it, "proceed across multiple

domains simultaneously". A medical response to depression is unlikely to be effective on its own. What is also required is a range of approaches that are geared to reducing stress and/or shoring up protective factors.

Whatever models of care are developed, what should underpin them is a person-centred approach that places the emphasis on identifying those features of loss and their meaning for the person, and developing a picture of the resources that people themselves can draw on and the coping strategies that have worked for them. This should be the starting point for developing action plans. These might include such diverse responses as individual and group exercise programmes to sustain/improve functional ability and heighten mood; pain management strategies; creative ways of bringing the person's social world to them (befriending, small neighbourhood networks, friendship/ support/activity groups around common interests); and support to enable people to resume activities of daily living (encouraging people to get out and about) as well as specific treatment and therapy for the depression.

Service delivery and practice

Reflecting on the reality of the service for the management and treatment of depression, Banerjee (1998) concludes that it seems to be "broke" as far as the needs of older people are concerned. With only around 6% of older people with serious depression within specialist psychiatric services and less than 15% of those with clinical level severity receiving any form of active management in primary care, the needs of older people with depression, he suggests, are not being met within the existing service systems. The evidence we have presented in this report reinforces and supports his observation.

At every level across health and social care services, older people with depression are relatively invisible. The most obvious and stark expression of this invisibility is in primary care. It is not simply that later life depression is not identified by GPs – even when diagnosed, it is generally not treated. When it is treated, this is often inappropriate. The gaps along the pathway from illness to recognition to treatment are reflected not only in primary care but also in other systems such as social care and supported housing.

Older people with depression do not get into specialist mental health services either. While those with more severe problems are more likely to be referred to such services, this is only the tip of a very large iceberg of potential need that can be ameliorated with appropriate help and support.

Specialist mental health services are never likely to be able to respond at the individual level to the full extent of need experienced by older people with mental health problems. It is inevitable that most of those with depression will continue to be supported within general medical and social services. If the service system is to 'get fixed', older people with depression must be made visible, and ways of enhancing the skills and expertise of generic workers across agencies and services must be found. These would need to encompass training, support and encouragement for staff to:

- increase awareness of later life depression and how it can be recognised;
- develop an understanding of risk and vulnerability factors implicated in its onset; and
- try out innovative and creative approaches to respond to it.

There is evidence of effective models of joint working between specialist mental health services and staff within generic services. These need to be explored and expanded.

The same kind of thinking needs to pervade policy and service development initiatives that are intended to support independence and well-being in older age. For example, key initiatives such as intermediate care have given little consideration to the specific needs of older people with depression. Our own ongoing research and experience of practice indicates that this is a prime area of unmet need. Moreover, what is known about risk and vulnerability to depression among older people suggests that models of rehabilitation must take into account, and respond to, the psychological impact of loss. There is a need to develop approaches that focus on strategies to manage

loss, mobilise resources to facilitate engagement in social life and support people in sustaining those things that are important to their sense of well-being. At the same time, the rehabilitation process is likely to take longer when the person is also depressed.

The challenge, therefore, is not to further compartmentalise older people's mental health problems in terms of service delivery systems but to use the accumulated understanding of the iterative, cumulative and interactive nature of those problems to develop appropriate responses within diverse spheres. This is not to suggest that there is no need for specialist provision. On the contrary, specialist services and expertise are required to treat those with the most severe and intractable problems, and to support generic services and staff in developing a more effective practice with older people with depression. But across specialist and generic services, the nature and extent of mental health problems among older people requires multi-level and multi-dimensional action.

From treating depression to supporting well-being

This report proposes the development of programmes to address multiple domains simultaneously to secure and sustain recovery in later life depression and to promote well-being over the ageing process. These need to start from an understanding of the ageing process and what it is that older people value in terms of well-being. The socio-cultural model of ageing, linked with an evidence-based approach on what is important to older people, provides a framework for developing locally based preventative strategies that address severally and together risk and resources at the individual, locality, local authority and community levels – in a partnership with older people.

References

Alexopoulos, G. and Chester, J. (1992) 'Outcomes of geriatric depression', *Clinics in Geriatric Medicine*, vol 8, no 3, pp 363-76.

Alexopoulos, G., Katz, I., Reynolds, C. and Ross, R. (2001) *Depression in older adults: A guide for patients and families*, New York, NY: CNS Inc.

Ames, D. (1993) 'Depressive disorders among elderly people in long-term institutional care', *Australia and New Zealand Journal of Psychiatry*, vol 27, no 3, pp 379-91.

Anderson, D. (2001) 'Treating depression in old age: the reasons to be positive', *Age and Ageing*, vol 30, no 1, pp 13-17.

Antonucci, T., Lansford, J., Akiyama, H., Smith, J., Baltes, M.M., Takahashi, K., Fuhrer, R. and Dartiques, J.F. (2002) 'Differences between men and women in social relations, resource deficits and depressive symptomatology during later life in four nations', *Journal of Social Issues*, vol 58, no 4, pp 767-83.

APA (American Psychiatric Association) (1994) *Diagnostic and statistical manual of mental disorders* (4th edn) (DSM-IV), Washington, DC: APA.

Arber, S. and Ginn, J. (1991) *Gender and later life: A sociological analysis of resources and constraints*, London: Sage Publications.

Arean, P.A. and Cook, B. (2002) 'Psychotherapy and combined psychotherapy/pharmacotherapy for late life depression', *Biological Psychiatry*, vol 52, no 3, pp 293-303.

Arean, P.A., Robinson, G. and Hicks, S. (1997) 'Mental illness in minority elderly: prevalence and use of services', presented at the 50th Annual Scientific Meeting of the Geriatric Society of America, November 1997.

Arie, T. and Jolley, D. (1982) 'Making services work: organisation and style of psycho-geriatric services', in R. Levy and F. Post (eds) *The psychiatry of late life*, Oxford: Blackwell Scientific Publications.

Audit Commission (2000) *Forget me not: Mental health services for older people*, London: Audit Commission.

Audit Commission (2002) *Audit Commission update: Forget me not 2002*, London: Audit Commission.

Bagley, H., Cordingley, L., Burns, A., Mozley, C.G., Sutcliffe, C., Challis, D. and Huxley, P. (2000) 'Recognition of depression by staff in nursing and residential homes', *Journal of Clinical Nursing*, vol 9, no 3, pp 445-50.

Baltes, P. and Baltes, M. (1990) *Successful ageing: perspectives from the behavioural sciences*, Cambridge: Cambridge University Press.

Baltes, M. and Carstensen, L. (1996) 'The process of successful ageing', *Ageing and Society*, vol 16, no 4, pp 397-422.

Baltes, P. and Mayer, K. (1999) *The Berlin Ageing Study*, Cambridge: Cambridge University Press.

Banerjee, S. (1998) 'Needs of special groups: the elderly', *International Review of Psychiatry*, vol 10, no 2, pp 130-3.

Banerjee, S. and Macdonald, A. (1996) 'Mental disorder in an elderly home care population: associations with health and social services use', *The British Journal of Psychiatry*, vol 168, no 8, pp 750-6.

Banerjee, S., Shamash, K., Macdonald, A. and Mann, A.H.(1996) 'Randomised controlled trial of effect of intervention by psycho-geriatric team on depression in frail elderly people at home', *British Medical Journal*, vol 313, no 7064, pp 1058-61.

Barlow, J. and Hainsworth, J. (2001) 'Volunteerism among older people with arthritis', *Ageing and Society*, vol 21, no 2, pp 203-317.

Beekman, A., Copeland, J. and Prince, M. (1999) 'Review of community prevalence of depression in later life', *The British Journal of Psychiatry*, vol 174, no 4, pp 307-11.

Beekman, A., Deeg, D., Braam, A., Smit, J. and Van Tilburg, W. (1997a), 'Consequences of major and minor depression in later life: a study of disability, well-being and service utilization', *Psychological Medicine*, vol 27, no 6, 1397-409.

Beekman, A., Deeg, D., Van Tilburg, T., Smit, J.H., Hooijer, C. and Van Tilburg, W. (1995) 'Major and minor depression in later life: a study of prevalence and risk factors', *Journal of Affective Disorders*, vol 36, no 1, pp 65-75.

Beekman, A., Penninx, B., Deeg, D., Ormel, J., Braam, A. and Van Tilburg, W. (1997b) 'Depression and physical health in later life: results from the Longitudinal Aging Study Amsterdam (LASA)', *Journal of Affective Disorders*, vol 46, no 3, pp 219-31.

Berkman, L. (2000) 'Social support, social networks, social cohesion and health', *Social Work in Health Care*, vol 31, no 2, pp 3-14.

Berkman, L. and Syme, L. (1979) 'Social networks, host resistance and mortality: a nine-year follow-up of Alameda County residents', *American Journal of Epidemiology*, vol 109, no 2, pp 186-204.

Bird, M. and Parslow, R. (2002) 'Potential for community programs to prevent depression in older people', *Medical Journal of Australia*, vol 177, no 7, pp S107-S110.

Blanchard, M.R., Waterreus, A. and Mann, A. (1994) 'The nature of depression among older people in inner London and the contact with primary care', *British Journal of Psychiatry*, vol 164, no 3, pp 396-402.

Bland, R.C., Newman, S.C. and Orn, H. (1988) 'Prevalence of psychiatric disorders in the elderly in Edmonton', *Acta Psychiatrica Scandinavica*, vol 77, (Suppl. 338), pp 57-63.

Blazer, D. (1993) *Depression in late life* (2nd edn), St Louis, Mississippi: Mosby-Year Book.

Blazer, D. (1996) 'Epidemiology of psychiatric disorders in late life', in E.W. Busse and D.G. Blazer (eds) *The American Psychiatric Press textbook of geriatric psychiatry* (2nd edn), Washington, DC: American Psychiatric Press, pp 155-71.

Blazer, D. (2000) 'Psychiatry and the oldest old', *American Journal of Psychiatry*, vol 157, no 12, pp 1915-24.

Bowling, A. (1994) 'Social networks and social support among older people and implications for emotional well-being and psychiatric morbidity', *International Review of Psychiatry*, vol 6, no 1, pp 41-58.

Bowling, G., Farquar, M. and Browne, P. (1991) 'Life satisfaction and associations with social network and support variables', *International Journal of Geriatric Psychiatry*, vol 6, no 6, pp 549-66.

Brilman, E. and Ormel, J. (2001) 'Life events, difficulties and onset of depressive episodes in later life', *Psychological Medicine*, vol 31, no 5, pp 859-69.

Brown, G. (1992) 'Life events and social support: possibilities for primary prevention', in R. Jenkins, J. Newton and R. Young (eds) *The prevention of depression and anxiety*, London: HMSO.

Brown, G. and Harris, T. (1978) *Social origins of depression: A study of psychiatric disorder in women*, London: Tavistock.

Brown, M., Lapane, K. and Luisi, A. (2002) 'The management of depression in older nursing home residents', *Journal of the American Geriatrics Society*, vol 50, no 1, pp 69-76.

Bruce, M., McAvay, G., Raue, P.J. and Brown, E. (2002) 'The epidemiology of major depression in elderly home health care patients', *American Journal of Psychiatry*, vol 159, no 8, pp 1367-74.

Byrne, G.J.A. and Raphael, B. (1994) 'A longitudinal study of bereavement phenomena in recently widowed elderly men', *Psychological Medicine*, vol 24, no 2, pp 411-21.

Callahan, C.M. (2001) 'Quality improvement research on late life depression in primary care', *Medical Care*, vol 39, no 8, pp 772-84.

Callahan, C.M., Hui, S.L., Nienaber, N.A., Musick, B. and Tierney, W. (1994) 'Longitudinal study of depression and health service use among elderly primary care patients', *Journal of the American Geriatrics Society*, vol 42, no 7, pp 833-8.

Cattan, M. (2002) *Supporting older people to overcome social isolation and loneliness*, London: Help the Aged/British Gas.

Chappell, N. (1999) *Volunteering and healthy aging: What we know*, Canada: Volunteering Canada.

Chappell, N. and Prince, M. (1994) *Voluntary action by seniors in Canada*, Victoria, Canada: Centre for Ageing, University of Victoria.

Coleman, P., Ivani-Chalian, C. and Robinson, M. (1993) 'Self esteem and its sources: stability and change in later life', *Ageing and Society*, vol 13, no 2, pp 171-92.

Coleman, P., Ivani-Chalian, C. and Robinson, M. (1998) 'The story continues: persistence of life themes in old age', *Ageing and Society*, vol 18, no 3, pp 389-419.

Copeland, J.R.M. (1999) 'Depression in older age: diagnostic problems, new knowledge and neglected areas', in M. Maj and N. Sartorius (eds) *Depressive disorders*, WPA Series: Evidence and experience in psychiatry, Chichester: John Wiley & Sons, pp 364-6.

Copeland, J.R.M., Chen, R., Dewey, M., McCracken, C.F.M., Gilmore. C., Larkin, B. and Wilson, K.C.M. (1999c) 'Community-based case-control study of depression in older people: cases and sub-cases from the MRC-ALPHA study', *The British Journal of Psychiatry*, vol 175, no 4, pp 340-7.

Copeland, J.R.M., Gurland, B.J., Dewey, M., Wood, N., Searle, R., Davidson, I.A. and McWilliam, C. (1987) 'The range of mental illness among the elderly in the community: prevalence in Liverpool using the GMS-AGECAT package', *British Journal of Psychiatry*, vol 150, no 6, pp 815-23.

Copeland, J.R.M., Beekman, A., Dewey, M., Jordan, A., Lawlor, B.A., Linden, M., Lobo, A., Magnusson, H., Mann, A., Fichter, M., Prince, M.J., Saz, P., Turrina, C. and Wilson, K.C.M. (1999b) 'Cross-cultural comparison of depressive symptoms in Europe does not support stereotypes of ageing', *The British Journal of Psychiatry*, vol 174, no 4, pp 322-9.

Copeland, J.R.M., Beekman, A., Dewey, M., Hooijer, C., Jordan, A., Lawlor, B.A., Lobo, A., Magnusson, H., Mann, A., Meller, I., Prince, M.J., Reischies, F., Turrina, C., de Vries, M.W. and Wilson, K.C.M. (1999a) 'Depression in Europe: geographical distribution among older people', *The British Journal of Psychiatry*, vol 174, no 4, pp 312-21.

Coyne, J. and Katz, I. (2001) 'Improving the primary care treatment of late life depression', *Medical Care*, vol 39, no 8, pp 756-9.

Crawford, M., Prince, M., Menezes, P. and Mann, A.H. (1998) 'The recognition and treatment of depression in older people in primary care', *International Journal of Geriatric Psychiatry*, vol 13, no 3, pp 172-6.

Creer, C., Sturt, L. and Wykes, T. (1982) 'The role of relatives in long term community care: experience in a London borough', in J. Wing (ed) *Psychological Medicine*, Monograph Supplement No 2, pp 3-55.

Cuijpers, P. and van Lammeren, P. (2001) 'Secondary prevention of depressive symptoms in elderly inhabitants of residential homes', *International Journal of Geriatric Psychiatry*, vol 16, no 7, pp 702-8.

Davis, M., Moye, J. and Karel, M. (2002) 'Mental health screening of older adults in primary care', *Journal of Mental Health and Aging*, vol 8, no 2, pp 139-49.

De Beurs, E., Beekman, A., Geerlings, S., Deeg, D., Van Dyck, R. and Van Tilburg, W (2001) 'On becoming depressed or anxious in late life: similar vulnerability factors but different effects of stressful life events', *The British Journal of Psychiatry*, vol 179, no 5, pp 426-31.

DH (Department of Health) (2001) *National service framework for older people*, London: DH.

Dimond, M., Caserta, M. and Lund, D. (1995) 'Understanding depression in bereaved older adults', *Clinical Nursing Research*, vol 3, no 3, pp 253-68.

Ebrahim, S., Patel, N., Coats, M., Greig, C., Gilley, J., Bangham, C. and Stacey, S. (1991) 'Prevalence and severity of morbidity among Gujarati Asian elders: a controlled comparison', *Family Practice*, vol 8, no 1, pp 57-62.

Fadden, G., Bebbington, P. and Kuipers, L. (1987) 'The burden of care: the impact of functional psychiatric illness on the patient's family', *British Journal of Psychiatry*, vol 15 , no 5, pp 660-7.

Farran, C.J., Horton-Deutsch, S.L., Loukissa, D. and Johnson, L. (1998) 'Psychiatric home care of elderly persons with depression: unmet caregiver needs', *Home Health Care Services Quarterly*, vol 16, no 4, pp 57-73.

Flint, A.J. and Rifat, S.L. (1997) 'The effect of treatment on the two year course of late life depression, *British Journal of Psychiatry*, vol 170, no 3 , pp 268-72.

Flint, A.J. and Rifat, S.L. (2000) 'Maintenance treatment for recurrent depression in late life: a four year outcome study', *American Journal of Geriatric Psychiatry*, vol 8, no 2, pp 150-9.

Freudenstein, U., Jagger, C., Arthur, A. and Donner-Banzhoff, N. (2001) 'Treatments for late life depression in primary care – a systematic review', *Family Practice*, vol 18, no 3, pp 321-7.

Friedhoff, A.J. (1994) 'Consensus development conference statement: diagnosis and treatment of depression in late life', in L.S. Schneider, C.F. Reynolds, B.D. Lebbowitz and A.J. Friedhoff (eds) *Diagnosis and treatment of depression in late life: Results of the NIH consensus development conference*, Washington, DC: American Psychiatric Press.

Fry, P. (1997) 'Grandparent's reactions to the death of a grandchild: an exploratory factor analytic study', *Omega: Journal of Death and Dying*, vol 35, no 1, pp 119-40.

Gallagher-Thompson, D., Futterman, A., Farberow, N., Thompson, L.W. and Peterson, J. (1993) 'The impact of spousal bereavement on older widows and widowers', in M.S. Stroebe, W. Stroebe and R.O. Hansson (eds), *Handbook of bereavement: Theory, research and intervention, USA*, New York, NY: Cambridge University Press.

Gallo, T.J., Rabins, P.V. and Anthony, J.C. (1999) 'Sadness in older persons: 13 year follow-up of a community sample in Baltimore, Maryland', *Psychological Medicine*, vol 29, no 2, pp 341-50.

Geiselmann, B., Linden, M. and Helmchen, H. (2001) 'Psychiatrists diagnoses of sub-threshold depression in old age: frequency and correlates', *Psychological Medicine*, vol 31, no 1, pp 51-63.

Gilbody, S. and Whitty, P. (2002) *Effective health care: Improving the recognition and management of depression in primary care*, vol 7, no 5, University of York: NHS Centre for Reviews and Dissemination.

Godfrey, M. (1998) *Older people with mental health problems: A literature review*, Leeds: Nuffield Institute for Health.

Godfrey, M. (2001) 'Prevention: developing a framework for conceptualizing and evaluating outcomes of preventive services for older people', *Health and Social Care in the Community*, vol 9, no 2, pp 89-99.

Godfrey, M. and Townsend, J. (1995) *Intensive home treatment: Users' and carers' experiences of service and outcomes of care*, Working Paper 1: Evaluation of a community mental health service, Leeds: Nuffield Institute for Health.

Godfrey, M. and Randall, T. (2003) *Developing a locality based approach to prevention for older people*, Leeds: Nuffield Institute for Health.

Godfrey, M., Hardy, B. and Wistow, G. (2003) 'Integrated care for older people with dementia', in A. van Raak, I. Mur-Veeman, B. Hardy, M. Steenbergen and A. Paulus (eds) *Integrated care in Europe*, Amsterdam: Elsevier, pp 145-67.

Godfrey, M., Townsend, J. and Denby, T. (2004) *Building a good life for older people in local communities: Ageing in time and place*, York: Joseph Rowntree Foundation.

Goldberg, D. (1992) 'Early diagnosis and secondary prevention', in R. Jenkins, J. Newton and R. Young (eds) *The prevention of depression and anxiety*, London: HMSO.

Goldman, H., Rye, P. and Sirovatka, P. (1999) *Mental health: A report of the Surgeon General*, Washington, DC: Office of the Surgeon General.

Gottlieb, B. (1985) 'Social networks and social support: an overview of research, practice and policy implications', *Health Education Quarterly*, vol 12, no 1, pp 5-22.

Gottlieb, B. (1987) 'Using social support to protect and promote health', *Journal of Primary Prevention*, vol 8, nos 1 and 2, pp 49-70.

Gottlieb, B. (ed) (1997) *Coping with chronic stress*, New York, NY: Plenum.

Green, B., Copeland, J.R., Dewey, M., Sharma, V., Saunders, P.A., Davidson, I.A., Sullivan, C. and McWilliam, C. (1992) 'Risk factors for depression in elderly people: a prospective study', *Acta Psychiatrica Scandinavica*, vol 86, no 3, pp 213-17.

Gurland, B., Cross, P. and Katz, S. (1996) 'Epidemiological perspectives on opportunities for treatment of depression', *Archives Family Medicine*, vol 4, no 4, Suppl.1, pp 167-72.

Han, B. (2002) 'Depressive symptoms and self-rated health in community-dwelling older adults: a longitudinal study', *Journal of the American Geriatrics Society*, vol 50, no 9, pp 1549-56.

Hays, J.C., Saunders, W., Flint, E., Kaplan, B.H. and Blazer, D.G. (1997) 'Social support and depression as risk factors for loss of physical function in late life', *Ageing and Mental Health*, vol 1, no 3, pp 209-20.

Hays, J.C., Steffens, D., Flint, E., Bosworth, H. and George, L. (2001) 'Does social support buffer functional decline in elderly patients with unipolar depression?', *American Journal of Psychiatry*, vol 158, no 11, pp 1850-5.

Hegge, M. (1991) 'A qualitative retrospective study of coping strategies of newly widowed elderly: effects of anticipatory grieving on the caregiver', *American Journal of Hospice and Palliative Care*, vol 8, no 4, pp 28-34.

Henderson, A., Jorm, A., Mackinnon, A., Christensen, H., Scott, L.R., Korten, A.E. and Doyle-Phillips, C. (1993) 'The prevalence of depressive disorders and the distribution of depressive symptoms in later life: a survey using Draft ICD-10 and DSM-III-R', *Psychological Medicine*, vol 23, no 3, pp 719-29.

Henderson, A., Korten, A., Jacomb, P., Mackinnon, A., Jorm, A., Christensen, H. and Rodgers, B (1997) 'The course of depression in the elderly: a longitudinal community-based study in Australia', *Psychological Medicine*, vol 27, no 1, pp 119-29.

Herrmann, N., Black, S.E., Lawrence, J., Szekely, C. and Szalai, J.P. (1998) 'The Sunnybrook stroke study: a prospective study of depressive symptoms and functional outcomes', *Stroke*, vol 29, no 3, pp 618-24.

Hinrichsen, G.A., Hernandez, N. and Pollack, S. (1992) 'Difficulties and rewards in family care of the depressed older adult', *The Gerontologist*, vol 32, no 4, pp 486-92.

Hinrichsen, G.A. and Hernandez, N. (1995) 'Factors associated with recovery from and relapse into major depressive disorder in the elderly', *American Journal of Psychiatry*, vol 150, no 12, pp 1820-5.

Hinrichsen, G.A. and Zweig, R. (1994) 'Family issues in late-life depression', *Journal of Long-Term Home Health Care*, vol 13, no 3, pp 4-15.

Holahan, C.K., Holahan, C.J. and Belk, S.S. (1984) 'Adjustment in ageing: the roles of life stress hassles and self-efficacy', *Health Psychology*, vol 3, no 4, pp 315-28.

Jacob, S. (1996) 'The grief experience of older women whose husbands had hospice care', *Journal of Advanced Nursing*, vol 24, no 2, pp 280-6.

Jerrome, D. and Wenger, C. (1999) 'Stability and change in late life friendships', *Ageing and Society*, vol 19, no 6, pp 661-76.

Jorm, A. (2000) 'Does old age reduce the risk of anxiety and depression? A review of epidemiological studies across the age span', *Psychological Medicine*, vol 30, no 1, pp 11-22.

Kanner, A., Coyne, J.C., Schaefer, C. and Lazarus, R.S. (1981) 'Comparison of two modes of stress measurement: daily hassles and uplifts versus major life events', *Journal of Behavioural Medicine*, vol 4, no 1, pp 1-39.

Kaplan, G., Strawbridge, W., Carnacho, T. and Cohen, R. (1993) 'Factors associated with change in physical functioning in the elderly: a six year prospective study', *Journal of Aging and Health*, vol 5, no 2, pp 140-53.

Karel, M.J. and Hinrichsen, G. (2000) 'Treatment of depression in late life: psychotherapeutic interventions', *Clinical Psychology Review*, vol 20, no 6, pp 707-29.

Katon, W.J. (1995) 'Will improving detection of depression in primary care lead to improved depressive outcomes?', *General Hospital Psychiatry*, vol 17, no 1, pp 1-2.

Katz, I.R., Simpson, G.M., Curlick, S.M., Parmelee, P.A. and Muhly, C. (1990) 'Pharmacologic treatment of major depression for elderly patients in residential care settings', *Journal of Clinical Psychiatry*, vol 51, (Suppl) pp 41-7.

Kivela, S. and Pahkala, K. (2001) 'Depressive disorder as a predictor of physical disability in old age', *Journal of the American Geriatrics Society*, vol 49, no 3, pp 290-6.

Kivela, S., Kongas-Saviaro, P., Kimmo, P., Kesti, E. and Laippala, P. (1996) 'Health, health behaviour and functional ability predicting depression in old age: a longitudinal study', *International Journal of Geriatric Psychiatry*, vol 11, no 10, pp 871-7.

Knipscheer, C., Van Groenou, M., Leene, G.J.F., Beekman, A. and Deeg, D. (2000) 'The effect of environmental context and personal resources on depressive symptomatology in older age: a test of the Lawton model', *Ageing and Society*, vol 20, no 2, pp 183-202.

Kraaij, V. and De Wilde, J. (2001) 'Negative life events and depressive symptoms in the elderly: a life span perspective', *Aging and Mental Health*, vol 5, no 1, pp 84-91.

Lawton, M.P. (1980) 'Environmental change: the older person as initiator and responder', in N. Datan and N. Lohmann (eds) *Transitions of aging*, New York, NY: Academic Press, pp 171-97.

Lazarus, R.S. (1999) *Stress and emotion: A new synthesis*, London: Free Association Books.

Lazarus, R. and Delongis, A. (1983)
'Psychological stress and coping in aging',
Journal of American Psychology, vol 38, no 3, pp
245-54.

Lee, G. (1985) 'Kinship and social support of the
elderly: the case of the United States', *Ageing
and Society*, vol 5, no 1, pp 19-38.

Lee, G. and Ish-Kuntz, M. (1988) 'Social
interaction, loneliness and emotional well
being among the elderly', *Research on Ageing*,
vol 9, pp 459-82.

Lefley, H. (1987) 'Ageing parents as caregivers
of mentally adult children: an emerging social
problem', *Hospital and Community Psychiatry*,
vol 38, no 10, pp 1063-70.

Le Gory, M. and Fitzpatrick, K. (1992) 'The
effect of environmental context on elderly
depression', *Journal of Aging and Health*, vol 4,
no 4, pp 459-79.

Lenze, E., Dew, A., Mazumdar, S., Begley,
A.E., Cornes, C., Miller, M.D., Imber, S.D.,
Frank, E., Kupfer, D.J. and Reynolds, C.F.
(2002) 'Combined pharmacotherapy and
psychotherapy as maintenance treatment
for late-life depression: effects on social
adjustment', *American Journal of Psychiatry*, vol
159, no 3, pp 466-8.

Lin, N., Ye, X. and Ensel, W. (1999) 'Social
support and depressed mood: a structural
analysis', *Journal of Health and Social Behaviour*,
vol 40, no4, pp 344-59.

Lindesay, J., Briggs, K. and Murphy, E. (1989) 'The
Guy's/Age Concern survey: prevalence rates of
cognitive impairment, depression and anxiety
in an urban elderly community', *British Journal
of Psychiatry*, vol 155, no 3, pp 317-29.

Linzer, M., Spitzer, R., Kroenke, K., Williams,
J.B., Hahn, S., Brody, D. and deGruy, F. (1996)
'Gender, quality of life and mental disorders
in primary care: results from the PRIMR-MD
1000 Study', *American Journal of Medicine*, vol
101, no 5, pp 526-33.

Liptzin, B., Grob, M.C. and Eisen, S.V.
(1988) 'Family burden of demented and
depressed elderly psychiatric in-patients', *The
Gerontologist*, vol 28, no 3, pp 397-400.

Livingston, G., Yard, P., Beard, A. and Katona,
C. (2000b) 'A nurse-coordinated educational
initiative addressing primary care professionals'
attitudes to and problem solving in depression
in older people – a pilot study', *International
Journal of Geriatric Psychiatry*, vol 15, no 6, pp
401-5.

Livingston, G., Hawkins, A., Graham, N.,
Blizard, B. and Mann, A. (1990) 'The Gospel
Oak study: prevalence rates of dementia,
depression and activity limitation among
elderly residents in inner London', *Psychological
Medicine*, vol 20, no 1, pp 137-46.

Livingston, G., Watkin, V., Milne, B., Manela,
M.V. and Katona, C. (2000a) 'Who becomes
depressed? The Islington community study of
older people', *Journal of Affective Disorders*, vol
58, no 2, pp 125-33.

Llewellyn-Jones, R.H., Baikie, K.A., Smithers, H.,
Cohen, J., Snowdon, J., Tennant, C.C., Deeks,
J. and Juszczak, E. (1999) 'Multifaceted shared
care intervention for late life depression in
residential care: randomised controlled trial',
British Medical Journal, vol 319, no 7211, pp
676-82.

Long, A., Godfrey, M., Randall, T., Grant, M.
and Chapman, M (2002) *Effectiveness and
outcomes of preventive services for older people:
Risk factors, coping strategies and outcomes of
interventions in bereavement*, Leeds: Nuffield
Institute for Health.

Lund, D., Caserta, M. and Dimond, M. (1993)
The course of spousal bereavement in later
life, in M.S. Stroebe, W. Stroebe and R.O.
Hansson (eds) *Handbook of bereavement:
Theory, research and intervention*, *USA*, New
York, NY: Cambridge University Press.

Lynch, D., McGinnis, R., Nagel, R., Tamburrino,
M. and Smith, M.K. (2002) 'Depression and
associated physical symptoms: comparison
of geriatric and non-geriatric family practice
patients', *Journal of Mental Health and Aging*, vol
8, no 1, pp 29-35.

Lyness, J.M., King, D.A., Cox, C., Yoediono, Z., Caine, E.D. (1999) 'The importance of sub-syndromal depression in older primary care patients: prevalence and associated functional disability', *Journal of the American Geriatrics Society*, vol 47, no 6, pp 647-52.

McCarthy, B., Lesage, A., Brewin, C.R., Brugha, T.S., Mangen, S. and Wing, J.K. (1989) 'Need for care among the relatives of long term users of day care', *Psychological Medicine*, vol 19, no 3, pp 725-36.

McCracken, C., Boneham, J., Copeland, J.R., Williams, K.E., Wilson, K., Scott, A., McKibbin, P. and Cleave, N. (1997) 'Prevalence of dementia and depression among elderly people in black and ethnic minorities', *The British Journal of Psychiatry*, vol 171, no 3, pp 269-73.

McMurdo, M. and Rennie, L. (1993) 'A controlled trial of exercise by residents of old people's homes', *Age and Ageing*, vol 22, no 1, pp 11-15.

Mann, A., Graham, N. and Ashby, D. (1984) 'Psychiatric illness in residential homes for the elderly: a survey in one London Borough', *Age and Ageing*, vol 13, no 5, pp 257-65.

Mather, A., Rodriguez, C., Guthrie, M., McHarg, A., Reid, I. and McMurdo, E.T. (2002) 'Effects of exercise on depressive symptoms in older adults with poorly responsive depressive disorder: randomised controlled trial', *The British Journal of Psychiatry*, vol 180, no 5, pp 411-15.

Mendes de Leon, C.F., Kasl, S.V. and Jacobs, S. (1994) 'A prospective study of widowhood and changes in symptoms of depression in a community sample of the elderly', *Psychological Medicine*, vol 24, no 3, pp 613-24.

Mehta, K.M., Yaffe, K. and Covinsky, K.E. (2002) 'Cognitive impairment, depressive symptoms and functional decline in older people', *Journal of the American Geriatrics Society*, vol 50, no 6, pp 1045-50.

Michael, Y., Berkman, L., Colditz, G. and Kawachi, I. (2001) 'Living arrangements, social integration and change in functional health status', *American Journal of Epidemiology*, vol 153, no 2, pp 123-31.

Morgan, K., Dalloso, H.M., Arie, T., Byrne, E.J., Jones, R., and Waite, J. (1987) 'Mental health and psychological well being among the old and very old living at home', *British Journal of Psychiatry*, vol 150, no 6, pp 801-7.

Moxon, S., Lyne, K., Sinclair, I., Young, P. and Kirk, C. (2001) 'Mental health in residential homes: a role for care staff', *Ageing and Society*, vol 21, no 1, pp 71-93.

Murphy, E. (1982) 'Social origins of depression in old age', *The British Journal of Psychiatry*, vol 141, no 2, pp 135-42.

Murphy, E. (1983) 'The prognosis of depression in old age', *British Journal of Psychiatry*, vol 121, no 4, pp 394-404.

Murrell, S.A., Meeks, S. and Walker, J. (1991) 'Protective functions of health and self-esteem against depression in older adults facing illness or bereavement', *Psychology and Aging*, vol 6, no 3, pp 352-60.

Musick, M. and Wilson, J. (2003) 'Volunteering and depression: the role of psychological and social resources in different age groups', *Social Science and Medicine*, vol 56, no 2, pp 259-69.

Norris, F. and Murrell, S. (1990) 'Social support, life events, and stress as modifiers of adjustment to bereavement by older adults', *Psychology and Aging*, vol 5, no 3, pp 429-36.

Oman, D., Thoresen, C. and McMahon, K. (1999) 'Volunteerism and mortality among the community-dwelling elderly', *Journal of Health Psychology*, vol 4, no 3, pp 301-16.

OPCS (Office of Population, Censuses and Surveys) (2004) *Living in Britain No 31: Results from the 2002 General Household Survey*, London: The Stationery Office.

Oslin, D., Datto, C., Kallan, M., Katz, I.R., Edell, W.S. and TenHave, T. (2002) 'Association between medical comorbidity and treatment outcomes in late-life depression', *Journal of the American Geriatrics Society*, vol 50, no 5, pp 823-8.

Palsson, S., Ostling, S. and Skoog, I. (2001) 'The incidence of first-onset depression in a population followed from the age of 70 to 85', *Psychological Medicine*, vol 31, no 6, pp 1159-68.

Penninx, B., Deeg, D., Van Eijk, J., Beekman, A. and Guralnik, J. (2000) 'Changes in depression and physical decline in older adults: a longitudinal perspective', *Journal of Affective Disorders*, vol 61, no1, pp 1-12.

Penninx, B., Guralnik, J.M., Ferrucci, L., Simonsick, E., Dorly, J., Deeg, D. and Wallace, R. (1998) 'Depressive symptoms and physical decline in community dwelling older persons', *Journal of the American Medical Association*, vol 279, no 21, pp 1720-6.

Phillipson, C., Bernard, M., Phillips, J. and Ogg, J. (2001) *The family and community life of older people*, London: Routledge.

Pickard, S. (1994) 'Life after death: the experience of bereavement in South Wales', *Ageing and Society*, vol 14, no 2, pp 191-217.

Pincus, H., Davies, W. and McQueen, L. (1999) '"Sub-threshold" mental disorders: a review and synthesis of studies on minor depression and other "brand names"', *The British Journal of Psychiatry*, vol 174, no 4, pp 288-96.

Prigerson, H., Frank, E., Reynolds, C., George, C. and Kupfer, D. (1993) 'Protective psychosocial factors in depression among spousally bereaved elders', *The American Journal of Geriatric Psychiatry*, vol 1, no 4, pp 296-309.

Prince, M.J., Harwood, R., Thomas, A. and Mann, A. (1998) 'A prospective population-based cohort study of the effects of disablement and social milieu on the onset and maintenance of late-life depression. The Gospel Oak Project VII', *Psychological Medicine*, vol 28, no 2, pp 337-50.

Prince, M.J., Harwood, R., Blizard, R., Thomas, A. and Mann, A. (1997a) 'Impairment, disability and handicap as risk factors for depression in old age. The Gospel Oak Project V', *Psychological Medicine*, vol 27, no 2, pp 311-21.

Prince, M.J., Harwood, R., Blizard, R., Thomas, A. and Mann, A. (1997b) 'Social support deficits, loneliness and life events as risk factors for depression in old age', *Psychological Medicine*, vol 27, no 2, pp 323-32.

Prince, M.J., Beekman, A., Deeg, D., Fuhrer, R., Kivela, S., Lawlor, B.A., Lobo, A., Magnusson, H., Meller, I., Van Oyen, H., Reischies, F., Roelands, M., Skoog, I., Turrina, C. and Copeland, J. (1999a) 'Depression symptoms in late life assessed using the EURO-D scale: effect of age, gender and marital status in 14 European centres', *The British Journal of Psychiatry*, vol 174, no 4, pp 339-45.

Prince, M.J., Reischies, F., Beekman, A., Fuhrer, R., Jonker, C., Kivela, S., Lawlor, B.A., Lobo, A., Magnusson, H., Fichter, M., Van Oyen, H., Roelands, M., Skoog, I., Turrina, C. and Copeland, J.R. (1999b) 'Development of the EURO-D scale – a European Union initiative to compare symptoms of depression in 14 European centres', *The British Journal of Psychiatry*, vol 174, no 4, pp 330-8.

Qureshi, H. and Walker, A. (1989) *The caring relationship: Elderly people and their families*, Basingstoke: Macmillan Press.

Rait, G., Burns, A., Baldwin, R., Morley, M., Chew-Graham, C., St Leger, A. and Abas, M. (1999) 'Screening for depression in African-Caribbean elders', *Family Practice*, vol 16, no 6, pp 591-5.

Rapaport, M.H. and Judd, L.L. (1998) 'Minor depressive disorder and sub syndromal depressive symptoms: functional impairment and response to treatment', *Journal of Affective Disorders*, vol 48, no 2/3, pp 227-32.

Rattenbury, C. and Stones, M.J. (1989) 'A controlled evaluation of reminiscence and current topics discussion groups in a nursing home context', *The Gerontologist*, vol 29, no 6, pp 768-71.

Reynolds, C. and Kupfer, D. (1999) 'Depression and aging: a look to the future', *Mental Health and Aging*, vol 50, no 9, pp 1167-72.

Roberto, K. and Stanis, P. (1994) 'Reactions of older women to the death of their close friends', *Omega: Journal of Death and Dying*, vol 29, no 1, pp 17-27.

Roberts, R., Kaplan, G., Shema, S. and Strawbridge, W. (1997a) 'Does growing old increase the risk for depression?', *American Journal of Psychiatry*, vol 154, no 10, pp 1384-90.

Roberts, R., Kaplan, G., Shema, S. and Strawbridge, W. (1997b) 'Prevalence and correlates of depression in an ageing cohort', *Journals of Gerontology Series B, Psychological Sciences and Social Sciences*, vol 52B, no 5, pp S252-S258.

Rook, K.S. (1990) 'Social relationships as a source of companionship: implications for older adults' psychological well-being', in B.R. Sarason, I.G. Sarason and G.R. Pierce (eds) *Social support: An interactional view*, New York, NY: John Wiley & Sons, pp 243-67.

Rothera, I., Jones, R. and Gordon, C. (2002) 'An examination of the attitude and practice of general practitioners in the diagnosis and treatment of depression in older people', *International Journal of Geriatric Psychiatry*, vol 17, no 4, pp 354-8.

Saarela, T. and Engestrom, R. (2003) 'Reported differences in management strategies by primary care physicians and psychiatrists in older patients who are depressed', *International Journal of Geriatric Psychiatry*, vol 18, no 2, pp 161-8.

Scambler, S., Victor, C., Bond, J. and Bowling, A. (2001) 'Understanding the experiences and causes of loneliness in later life: constructing a sociological framework for conceptualising older people's experiences and definitions', Paper presented at the European Sociological Association Conference, Helsinki, September 2001.

Scharf, T., Phillipson, C. and Smith, A.E. (2002) *Growing older in socially deprived areas: Social exclusion in later life*, London: Help the Aged.

Schneider, J. (ed) (1997) *Quality of care: Testing some measures in homes for elderly people*, Discussion Paper 1245, Canterbury: Personal Social Services Research Unit, University of Kent at Canterbury.

Schoevers, R., Geerlings, M., Beekman, A., Penninx, B., Deeg, D., Jonker, C. and Van Tilburg, W. (2000) 'Association of depression and gender with mortality in old age', *The British Journal of Psychiatry*, vol 177, no 4, pp 336-42.

Seeman, T. (1995) 'Behavioural and psychosocial predictors of physical performance: Macarthur Studies of Successful Ageing', *Journal of Gerontology*, vol 50A, no 4, pp M177-M183.

Seeman, T. and Berkman, L. (1988) 'Structural characteristics of social networks and their relationship with social support in the elderly – who provides support', *Social Science and Medicine*, vol 26, no 7, pp 737-49.

Silveira, E. and Allebeck, P. (2001) 'Migration, ageing and mental health: an ethnographic study on perceptions of life satisfaction, anxiety and depression in older Somali men in East London', *International Journal of Social Welfare*, vol 10, no 4, pp 309-20.

Silveira, E. and Ebrahim, S. (1995) 'Mental health and health status of elderly Bengalis and Somalis in London', *Age and Aging*, vol 24, no 6, pp 474-80.

Sinclair, P., Lyness, J., King, D., Cox, C. and Caine, E. (2001) 'Depression and self-reported functional status in older primary care patients', *American Journal of Psychiatry*, vol 158, no 3, pp 416-19.

Smaje, C. (1995) *Health, race and ethnicity*, London: Kings Fund Institute.

Smith, J., Borchelt, M., Maier, H. and Jopp, D. (2002) 'Health and well-being in the young old and the oldest old', *Journal of Social Issues*, vol 58, no 4, pp 715-32.

Snowdon, J. (2001) 'Is depression more prevalent in old age?', *Australian and New Zealand Journal of Psychiatry*, vol 35, no 6, pp 782-7.

Soon, J. and Levine, M. (2002) 'Screening for depression in patients in long-term care facilities: a randomised controlled trial of physician response', *Journal of the American Geriatrics Society*, vol 50, no 6, pp 1092-9.

Stevens, T., Cornelius, K., Manela, M., Watkin, V. and Livingston, G. (1999) 'Drug treatment of older people with affective disorders in the community: lessons from an attempted clinical trial', *International Journal of Geriatric Psychiatry*, vol 14, no 4, pp 467-72.

Thoits, P. and Hewitt, L. (2001) 'Volunteer work and well-being', *Journal of Health and Social Behaviour*, vol 42, no 2, pp 115-31.

Thom, B., Waller, S. and Quigley, R. (2002) *Preventing and reducing depression in later life: Review of reviews*, London: Health Development Agency.

Timonen, L., Rantanen, T.E. and Sulkava, R. (2002) 'Effects of a group-based exercise program on the mood state of frail older women after discharge from hospital', *International Journal of Geriatric Psychiatry*, vol 17, no 12, pp 1106-11.

Tuma, T.A. (1996) 'Effect of age on the outcome of hospital treated depression', *The British Journal of Psychiatry*, vol 168, no 1, pp 76-81.

Turner, R.J., Lloyd, D. and Roszell, P. (1999) 'Personal resources and the social distribution of depression', *American Journal of Community Psychology*, vol 27, no 5, pp 543-672.

Unutzer, J. (2002) 'Diagnosis and treatment of older adults with depression in primary care', *Biological Psychiatry*, vol 52, no 3, pp 285-92.

Unutzer, J., Katon, W., Sullivan, M. and Miranda, J. (1999) 'Treating depressed older adults in primary care: narrowing the gap between efficacy and effectiveness', *The Milbank Quarterly*, vol 77, no 2, pp 225-51.

Walker, M., Orrell, M., Manela, M., Livingston, G. and Katona, C. (1998) 'Do health and use of services differ in residents of sheltered accommodation? A pilot study', *International Journal of Geriatric Psychiatry*, vol 13, no 9, pp 617-24.

Wasserburger, L., Arrington, D. and Abraham, I. (1996) 'Using elderly volunteers to care for the elderly: opportunities for nursing', *Nursing Economics*, vol 14, no 4, pp 232-8.

Wenger, G.C., Davies, R. and Shahtahmasebi, S. (1996) 'Social isolation and loneliness in old age: review and model refinement', *Ageing and Society*, vol 16, no 3, pp 333-58.

Weissman, M.M., Myers, J.K., Tischler, G.L., Holzer, C.E., Leaf, P.J., Orvaschel, H. and Brody, J.A. (1985) 'Psychiatric disorders (DSM-III) and cognitive impairment in the elderly in a US urban community', *Acta Psychiatrica Scandinavica*, vol 71, no. 4, pp 366-79.

Wernicke, T., Linden, M., Gillberg, R. and Helmchen, H. (2000) 'Ranges of psychiatric morbidity in the old and very old – results from the Berlin Aging Study (BASE)', *European Archives of Psychiatry and Clinical Neuroscience*, vol 250, no 3, pp 111-19.

WHO (World Health Organization)(1992) *The ICD-10 classification of mental and behavioural disorders: Clinical descriptions and diagnostic guidelines*, Geneva: WHO.

WHO (1993) *The ICD-10 classification of mental and behavioural disorders: Diagnostic criteria for research*, Geneva: WHO.

Young, A., Klap, R., Scherbourne, C. and Well, K. (2001) 'The quality of care for depressive and anxiety disorders in the United States', *Archives of General Psychiatra*, vol 58, no 1, pp 55-61.

Zarit, S., Femia, E., Gatz, M. and Johansson, B. (1999) 'Prevalence, incidence and correlates of depression in the oldest old: the OCTOC study', *Aging and Mental Health*, vol 3, no 2, pp 119-28.

Zisook, S. and Shuchter, S. (1991) 'Early psychological reaction to the stress of widowhood', *Psychiatry*, vol 54, no 4 , pp 320-33.

Zisook, S. and Shuchter, S. (1993) 'Major depression associated with widowhood', *American Journal of Geriatric Psychiatry*, vol 1, no 4, pp 316-26.

Appendix A: Search strategy

This was a scoping rather than a systematic review. We did not seek to critically assess the quality of the evidence base using explicit evaluative criteria. Rather, we sought to develop as comprehensive a picture of the nature of the evidence base as we could, within the limited resources available to us.

An initial scoping search of the following databases was carried out, using a combination of subject headings and freetext terms.

ASSIA (Applied Social Sciences Index and Abstracts)

Depression or late life depression and aged or elderly or geriatric and prevalence and risk

Social services abstracts

Sociological abstracts

Web of Science (Medline, Cinahl, Psychinfo)

Using the abstracts provided, articles identified as relevant to the topic of the review were retrieved and organised by theme – nature, prevalence, specific risk factors. The focus was primarily on research studies and reviews, although 'expert' policy statements relating to the nature and treatment of depression were also drawn on. From the articles retrieved, citations that also had a bearing on the review topic were sought.

Where this broad-based search strategy did not produce material (for example, retirement as a risk factor in later life depression), a further search of the same databases, using relevant thesaurus terms, was carried out.

In addition to the database searches, a hand search of relevant academic journals was also carried out for the period 1998 to 2003, namely:

Aging and Mental Health

Ageing and Society

Journal of Advanced Nursing

International Journal of Ethnicity and Ageing

American Journal of Psychiatry

Family Practice

British Journal of Psychiatry

Appendix B: Longitudinal studies on ageing

The Australian Longitudinal Study on Ageing (ALSA)

ALSA is a cross-disciplinary, prospective study of adults aged 70 and over that began in Adelaide, Australia in 1992. It is a population-based bio-psychosocial and behavioural study of 2,087 older adults in the community and in residential care.

The research aims to develop understanding of how social, biomedical and environmental factors are associated with age-related changes in the health and well-being of those aged 70 and over. Emphasis is given to the effects of social and economic factors on morbidity, disability, acute and long-term care service use, mortality and successful ageing.

Details and publications on:
www.cas.flinders.edu.au/alsa.html

The Berlin Ageing Study (BASE)

BASE is a multi-disciplinary, longitudinal study of 516 residents of West Berlin, aged 70-103, and living in both community and institutional settings. The study's theory, design and methods are geared to exploring the psychological, social and biomedical features of ageing, as well as the experience of ageing in a reasonably representative sample of adults across the age spectrum.

Details and publications on:
www.base-berlin.mpg.de/

The Bonn Longitudinal Study of Ageing (BOLSA)

BOLSA began in 1965 with a group of 222 older people. These comprised those born between 1890 and 1905 (108) and those born between 1900 and 1905 (114). Of the younger cohort, 55 were women and 59 were men. At each measurement point (there were seven between 1965 and 1984), three structured questionnaires were administered on different facets of people's lives. Participants also underwent a series of cognitive tests, including psychomotor and personality tests.

The Canberra Longitudinal Study

This study began in 1991 and completed its fourth wave at the end of 2002. The sample at baseline comprised 945 people aged 70 and over, living in the community. A further sample of 100 people living in institutions (special hostels for older people and nursing homes) was also included. Its specific focus is on the mental health of older people and the factors that impact on cognitive and functional mental health problems in older age.

Details and publications on:
www.anu.edu.au/cmhr/cls.php

The Longitudinal Ageing Study Amsterdam (LASA)

LASA is an interdisciplinary, longitudinal study over a period of at least 10 years. It started in 1991. The sample was constructed so as to reflect the national distribution of urbanisation and population density. It was drawn from three culturally distinct geographical areas in the west, north east and south of the Netherlands. Key issues of interest in the study are autonomy and quality of life of older people.

Details and publications on:
http://ssg.scw.vu.nl/lasa/

Lund 80+

Lund 80+ is a longitudinal study of older people, aged 80 and over in Lund, Sweden. It began in 1988. All those born in 1908 that belonged to one of Lund's six health care centres were invited to participate in the study. The ageing process of this group has been studied with yearly surveys, tests and interviews. In 1993, when this first cohort reached the age of 85, all people born in 1913 were invited to take part. In 1998, when the first cohort reached the age of 90 and the second reached 85, a third cohort born in 1918 was invited to participate. After this, a new cohort will be invited to take part every fifth year until everyone in the original cohort has died. Those born in 1913 and in subsequent cohorts are being studied only every fifth year.

Details and publications on:
www.geron.lu.se

Appendix C: A framework of risk and protective factors in securing life quality in ageing

Domain	Elements of life quality	Risk factors	Protective factors
Individual	Health (physical and mental health). Social relationships (sociability, companionship, intimacy, personal, emotional and instrumental support, stimulation, enjoyment) based on reciprocity and interdependence. Social activities (stimulating, fun, rewarding, interesting). 'Belonging' (social participation).	Loss of health. Disability and loss of functioning. Loss of role/purpose. Loss of place. Loss of intimates (bereavement, move). Loss of friends. Loss of connection/ belonging.	Orientation towards the future. Continuity of place. Adaptive coping strategies. Structure and composition of networks. Size of networks. Nature and quality of relationships and support. Opportunities for social participation. Interests, leisure.
Community	Participation and engagement. Quality of social environment. Quality of physical environment.	Lack of engagement. Inter- and intra-group mistrust. Poor physical/social environment. Crime (fear of and actual). Inadequate/inaccessible service provision.	Nature of community networks (composition, linkages, density, heterogeneity). Normative ties (trust, reciprocity, cooperation). Quality of social environment (safe/secure and participative). Opportunities to have one's voice heard at all levels.
National/ societal	Material resources for a 'comfortable' life. Inclusion (social and political life).	Poverty (lack of material resources). Structural inequality (life span perspective for individuals, groups, localities and communities). Unequal access to opportunities for social and political involvement.	Engagement in civic life. Civic identity. Action to reduce structural inequality.